GLOBETROTTER™

Travel

GW00708376

SRI LANKA

ROBIN GAULDIE

NEW
HOLLAND

NEW
HOLLAND

★★★ Highly recommended
★★ Recommended
★ See if you can

First edition published in 2000
by New Holland Publishers (UK) Ltd
London • Cape Town • Sydney • Auckland

10 9 8 7 6 5 4 3 2 1

24 Nutford Place
London W1H 6DQ
United Kingdom

80 McKenzie Street
Cape Town 8001
South Africa

14 Aquatic Drive
Frenchs Forest, NSW 2086
Australia

218 Lake Road
Northcote, Auckland
New Zealand

Distributed in the USA by
The Globe Pequot Press
Connecticut

ISBN 1 85368 815 0

Commissioning Editor: Tim Jollands
Manager Globetrotter Maps: John Loubser
Editors: Mary Duncan, Sara Harper
Picture Researchers: Carmen Watts, Colette Stott
Design and DTP: Michael Lyons
Cartographer: Carl Germishuys
Proofreader: Thea Grobbelaar

Reproduction by Hirt & Carter (Pty) Ltd, Cape Town
Printed and bound in Hong Kong by Sing Cheong
Printing Co. Ltd.

Photographic Credits:
Christine Osbourne Pictures: pages 6, 10, 11, 12, 13,
14, 16, 17, 22, 24, 25, 27 [top], 30, 31, 42, 43, 49, 54, 57,
59, 66, 81, 87, 100, 104, 105, 112, 118, 119 [bottom];
Gerald Cubitt: pages 46, 55, 56, 79;
Caroline Jones: cover, pages 69 [top], 82;
Peter Baker/PhotoBank: pages 7, 64, 65, 108;
Jeanetta Baker/PhotoBank: page 20;
Dominic Sansoni/ Christine Osbourne Pictures: title,
pages 4, 23, 28, 58, 62, 68, 83, 84, 90, 96 [top], 99, 102,
103, 116;
Jeroen Snijders: pages 8, 9, 15, 21, 26, 27 [bottom],
29, 32, 36, 37, 38, 39, 40, 41, 50, 51, 53, 69 [bottom], 71,
74, 76, 77, 78, 80, 85, 92, 95, 96 [bottom], 98, 107, 109,
110, 111;
Studio Times/Christine Osbourne Pictures: pages
114, 117, 119 [top].

Although every effort has been made to ensure
accuracy of facts, and telephone and fax numbers
in this book, the publishers will not be held
responsible for changes that occur at the time of
going to press.

Cover: *Glass-bottomed boat, Hambantota Beach.*
Title Page: *Tea pickers, Nuwara Eliya.*

CONTENTS

1
Introducing
Sri Lanka

Sri Lanka is an island of many names – all magically evocative of a **tropical land** of exotic spices, cool misty highlands, sun-soaked beaches, age-old temples and lost cities. To the ancient Greeks it was Taprobane; to the Arabs, Serendib; to later European conquerors, Ceilao, Zeylan or Ceylon; and in the Sinhala tongue of most of its own people, Sri Lanka – 'Lanka the Blessed'.

A teardrop-shaped island just off the southern tip of the Indian subcontinent, less than 50km (31 miles) away at its closest, Sri Lanka has links with the cultures of India that stretch back beyond history, but it would be a mistake to think of it as an India in miniature.

For the visitor, much of its enduring appeal stems from a near-unique combination of tropical sunshine and superb beaches with a fascinating and colourful culture epitomized by the mighty relics of ancient, vanished empires. All of this is concentrated within one tiny package, just 435km (270 miles) long and 225km (140 miles) at its widest, making it easy to experience much of the best of Sri Lanka within a relatively short time.

It's quite possible to pack into a two-week holiday a tour of the fascinating heritage sites of Anuradhapura, Sigiriya and Polonnaruwa (the so-called '**Cultural Triangle**'), a visit to the primal jungles of the Ruhuna National Park, two to three days of scuba diving on the south coast, and still have plenty of time left for lazy days on the beach, visiting botanical gardens, shopping for various arts and crafts, and sampling Sri Lanka's lip-smacking, spicy cuisine.

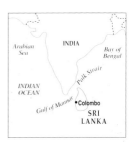

Top Attractions

*** **Kandy:** ancient hill capital with awesome Temple of the Buddha's Tooth.
*** **Anuradhapura:** ruined capital of Sri Lanka's greatest kingdom; being restored.
*** **Polonnaruwa:** fantastic 1000-year-old ruined city.
*** **Sigiriya:** cliff-top citadel with superb views and 1700-year-old rock paintings.
*** **Ruhuna (Yala):** elephants, leopard and rich bird-life in huge national park.
** **Galle:** evocative remnants of Dutch colonial period within massive fortress walls.

Opposite: *Sigiriya is one of the most striking sights in Sri Lanka.*

FACT FILE

Geography: has a total land area of 62,705km² (24,204 sq miles) and is 435km (270 miles) from north to south and 225km (140 miles) from east to west at its widest.
Highest point: at 2524m (8281ft), it is Pidurutalagala.
Government: it became independent from Britain in 1948. Executive power rests with elected president, balanced by single-house elected parliament.
Population: roughly 19 million, of whom around 72 per cent are Sinhalese, 20 per cent Tamil, 8 per cent 'Moors' or Malays and fewer than 1 per cent of other ethnic or religious groups.

Below: *The steep, jungle-cloaked highlands of Sri Lanka's hill country repelled colonial intruders until the 19th century.*

THE LAND

Sri Lanka lies 10 degrees north of the Equator and south and east of India, separated from it by the Gulf of Mannar, Palk's Bay and Palk Strait, which at its narrowest point, between the Indian mainland and the Jaffna Peninsula, is less than 80km (50 miles) wide. The sea crossing between Rameswaram, in India, and Mannar Island, off the northwest coast of Sri Lanka, is only around 32km (20 miles).

There is evidence of a natural land bridge connecting Sri Lanka with India at this point, and indeed this vanished causeway, only a few metres below sea level, is still known as **Adam's Bridge**. This close proximity to the subcontinent has meant that Sri Lanka's history and ecology have always been exposed to strong influences from its larger neighbour.

Gemstones, Citadels and Rivers

Geologically, Sri Lanka is composed of gneiss, schist, granite, quartzite and crystalline limestone – an agglomeration that generated **rich gemstone deposits**, washed by streams and rivers from the central highlands into lowland valleys. For more than 2000 years Sri Lanka has been a noted producer of rubies, sapphires, and semi-precious stones such as amethyst, alexandrite and topaz.

From a coastal plain, the island rises to an area of south-central highlands, which reach their highest point at **Pidurutalagala** (2524m / 8281ft). As European conquerors – first the Portuguese, followed by the Dutch and finally the British – tightened their grip on the island, this hard-to-reach hill country became the final fastness of Sri Lanka's last independent rulers, the kings of Kandy. In even earlier times, they provided a refuge for island kingdoms assaulted by invaders from southern India, and as a result the hill country has the most impressive concentration of once-mighty cities, fortresses and temples in the country.

Two major rivers flow out of the highlands – the **Mahaweli**, which flows northeast to reach the Indian Ocean near Trincomalee, and the **Walawe**, which joins the ocean near Hambantota on the south coast. A third, the **Aruvi**, flows out of the northern fringes of the highlands and the dry zone which surrounds them, emptying into Palk Bay on the northwest coast.

Above: *The ruined city of Polonnaruwa – monument to a vanished Lankan civilization – is one of the most evocative sites on the island.*

Harbours and Beaches

Sri Lanka's natural harbours have made the island a magnet for mariners throughout its history, from the legendary **Sindbad the Sailor** to the Portuguese navigator **Vasco da Gama** and the others who followed in search of the untold wealth of the fabled Orient. Modern visitors are as likely to be drawn by some 1600km (994 miles) of sandy beaches, warm Indian Ocean waters and coral reefs.

Colombo, the capital, lies on the west coast and is home to some 800,000 of Sri Lanka's approximately 19 million population. Relatively few Sri Lankans are city-dwellers; of the country's other cities, none approach

MAJOR CITIES
Colombo: 800,000 (1999 estimate)
Kandy: 147,000
Negombo: 140,000
Beruwala: 136,000
Ratnapura: 109,000
Polonnaruwa: 106,000
Nuwara Eliya: 103,000
Hikkaduwa: 97,000
Galle: 97,000
Bentota: 48,000

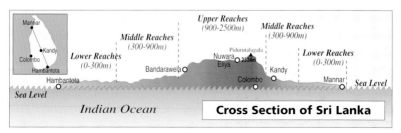

Cross Section of Sri Lanka

even Colombo's modest size. The most popular beach resorts are those closest to the capital: **Negombo**, only 35km (22 miles) north and close to the international airport, is a thriving resort and residential community of some 140,000 people. About 55–65km (30–40 miles) south of the capital, **Beruwala** and **Bentota**

Above: *Sun-seekers are drawn to the beaches of Sri Lanka's southwest, such as Hikkaduwa, one of the island's most popular holiday resort areas.*

Opposite: *The rainforests around Kandy in the central hill country region shelter hundreds of birds.*

have merged into the island's biggest resort area, with international-standard resort hotels, restaurants and watersports, and form the gateway to a 130km (80-mile) stretch of beaches which display varying degrees of tourism development, with **Hikkaduwa**, 100km (62.5 miles) south of Colombo, forming a second resort hub. Close to the southern end of this tourism ribbon, and on the southwest corner of the island, **Galle**, with a population of 97,000, is the most important town in southern Sri Lanka. The south coast is less thoroughly developed, though its excellent surf, beaches and dive sites have for long attracted younger and independent travellers, scuba divers and surfers.

Climate

Only 640km (500 miles) north of the equator, Sri Lanka's **tropical** climate shows little seasonal variation in temperature. Around the coasts, temperatures hover between 26°C (78°F) and 28°C (82°F), with a mean temperature in the capital of 27.5°C (81.5°F). Inland, however, average

COMPARATIVE CLIMATE CHART	COLOMBO				EAST COAST				KANDY			
	WIN	SPR	SUM	AUT	WIN	SPR	SUM	AUT	WIN	SPR	SUM	AUT
	JAN	APR	JULY	OCT	JAN	APR	JULY	OCT	JAN	APR	JULY	OCT
MIN TEMP. °C	22	24	25	24	24	26	26	24	8	9	13	11
MAX TEMP. °C	30	31	29	29	27	32	33	31	19	22	18	20
MIN TEMP. °F	72	75	77	75	75	78	78	75	47	49	55	52
MAX TEMP. °F	86	88	85	85	80	89	92	88	67	71	65	68
HOURS OF SUN	8	7	6	7	8	7	6	7	8	7	6	7
RAINFALL mm	89	231	135	348	173	58	51	221	170	119	300	269
RAINFALL in	3.5	9.1	5.3	13.7	6.8	2.3	2.0	8.7	6.7	4.7	11.8	10.6
DAYS OF RAINFALL	7	14	12	19	10	5	3	13	13	15	25	22

temperatures are very much cooler. From May to September, the **southwest monsoon** deposits heavy rain on the south and west coasts, from Colombo to Galle and points east, and also raises heavy seas which make swimming and diving unattractive. The worst intensity of the monsoon generally passes by late July or early August. The north and east, including the main east coast port of Trincomalee, are affected by the **northeast monsoon** from November to February, but this will have little impact on most visitors, as the main resort areas and visitor attractions are concentrated in the south and the central hills. Local thunderstorms can occur at any time of year, and while these are often intense they do not usually last more than a few hours.

Fauna

Encompassing habitats which range from dry zone scrub, mangrove swamp, and lowland rain forest to cloud forest and cultivated land, Sri Lanka is among Asia's most **biologically diverse** countries.

Sri Lanka is rich in wildlife, which has at least partly been protected by the Buddhist taboo on the taking of life. This provides little protection, however, against habitat destruction, and the country's many national parks and wildlife reserves probably play a

National Parks

INDIAN OCEAN

Kankasanturai • Point Pedro

Jaffna

Chundikkulam Sanctuary

Kilinochchi   • Mullaittivu

0   20 km

0   10 miles

Madhu Road Sanctuary

Chundikula & Kokkilai Bird Sanctuary

Mannar

Giant's Tank Sanctuary   • Vavuniya

Naval Headquarters Sanctuary   • Trincomalee

N

Wilpattu National Park   **Anuradhapura**   Mutur

Somawathie Chaitiya Sanctuary

Ritigala Strict Natural Reserve

Trikonamadu Natural Reserve

• Puttalam

Minneriya Giritale Sanctuary   • Polonnaruwa

Wasgomuwa Strict Natural Reserve

Batticaloa

Chilaw •

Maduru Oya National Park

Kurunegala •   • Matale

Kandy •   Gal Oya National Park   Ampara

Kegalla

Sakamam Sanctuary

Victoria Randenigala Rantambe Sanctuary

Negombo •

Gampaha   Nuwara Eliya   **Badulla**

Lahugala National Park   • Pottuvil

COLOMBO •   Galway's Land Sanctuary

Peak Wilderness Sanctuary

Panadura •

Ratnapura   Uda Walawe National Park   Yala National Park   Yala East National Park

Beruwala •

Kumana Bird Sanctuary

Bentota •

Sinharaja Biosphere Reserve   Wirawila Tissa Bird Sanctuary   Ruhuna National Park

Hambantota •   Bundala National Park

Galle •   Weligama

INDIAN OCEAN   Matara   • Tangalla

Below: *One of Sri Lanka's several species of kingfisher perches in an allspice tree.*

more important part in ensuring the survival of endemic bird and animal species. Among the most exciting and accessible of the national parks is **Ruhuna (Yala)**, 309km (190 miles) southeast of Colombo and covering some 1259km² (486 sq miles) of open plains, dense jungle, and Indian Ocean shoreline. Large numbers of wild elephants may still be found here and in the adjoining **Lahugala Elephant Sanctuary**.

Orphaned young elephants whose parents have been the victims of poachers or accidents are cared for at the **Elephant Orphanage**, on the main Colombo–Kandy road. Other large mammal species include wild buffalo, whose domesticated relatives can often be seen ploughing or pulling carts; five deer species, including sambur, spotted deer, hog deer, red deer and mouse deer; and the island's only bear species, the elusive sloth bear, found in lowland forests. Monkeys include the red macaque, grey langur, leaf monkey and bear monkey, as well as the slow-moving nocturnal loris; and the squirrel family includes the small palm squirrel, flying squirrel, and giant squirrel. Reptiles include two types of crocodile, the river crocodile and marsh crocodile; several species of monitor, gecko and chameleon; and more than 80 snake species, among them the cobra, which often appears in Buddhist and Hindu mythology.

Offshore, Sri Lanka is ringed by a **wide coral shelf**. While this has not escaped the degradation that has affected coral reefs worldwide, it still provides superb diving, sheltering fish species including emperor angel, moorish idol, powder-blue surgeon, sergeant-major, lion fish, unicorn fish, and a variety of parrot fish species. Pelagic species and game fish include marlin, pompano, ranax, yellowfin and barracuda, jack, and dog-tooth tuna. Sea mammals sighted off the east coast can include sperm whale, Bryde's whale and Indian Ocean dolphin, and even blue whale have occasionally been seen.

Plant Life

As with its fauna, Sri Lanka's wide **range of habitats** provides niches for a bewildering array of plant species, from shoreline plants like mangrove to rainforest giants, succulents and thorn trees adapted to live in the dry zone, and tiny high-altitude species capable of finding a place among rocky peaks and bare boulders. Sri Lanka is still well forested, with more than 8000 ha (19768 acres) of virgin, uninhabited woodland in the Sinharaja Forest alone. Sinharaja is reputed to shelter some 120 tree species, including ironwood, satinwood, teak, ebony and flamboyant. The '**bo-**' or '**bodhi tree**' (*Ficus religiosa*), a species of fig, is sacred to the Lord Buddha and is found throughout the island. Rhododendron forests grow on the hillsides of the Horton Plains region. Cultivated trees include coconut palm, which yields oil, copra, desiccated coconut, and alcoholic 'arrack'. Rubber, introduced by the British as a cash crop, is grown below the 600m (1969ft)contour. Numerous **spices**, including cinnamon, pepper, cardamom, cloves and nutmeg, were among the treasures which first drew Arab and European traders to Sri Lanka. Visitors will find a delicious array of fresh fruit, from familiar varieties such as banana, papaya, pineapple, mango and guava to local seasonal varieties such as mangosteen, rambutan and the strong-smelling durian.

But perhaps the plant for which Sri Lanka is most famous is tea, which flourishes in the high country, growing well between 600m (1969ft) and 1800m (5906ft) above sea level. Tea from Sri Lanka – still mostly marketed under the name of '**Ceylon' tea** – is reckoned among the world's finest and a visit to a tea plantation is part of most sightseeing tours of the island.

Left: *Briliant blooms lend splashes of colour to Kandy's Peradeniya Botanical Gardens.*

MARINE TURTLES

Five species of marine turtle nest on Sri Lanka's beaches. All are **threatened** by loss of habitat due to encroaching tourism development and by the slaughter of adult turtles for meat and shell.

At Rekewa, 200km (124 miles) south of Colombo, the Turtle Conservation project set up in the late 1990s protects a 2km (1.2-mile) stretch of beach where all five species – loggerhead, leatherback, Olive Ridley, green and tortoiseshell – lay their eggs.

Above: *Ruins dating from as early as 300BC can be visited at Anuradhapura.*

HISTORY IN BRIEF

Early History

The earliest traces of human habitation in Sri Lanka date from the **Old Stone Age** of about 1,750,000 years ago, and archaeological evidence sug-gests that later hunter-gatherers wandered across a land bridge between the Indian sub-continent and Sri Lanka some 10,000 years ago. In the ancient Hindu epic, the *Ramayana*, Lanka (not yet blessed with the prefix 'Sri') appears as the homeland of the demon king Ravana, who kidnaps Siva, wife of the hero Rama.

The Maurya Empire

The earliest historical record is the remarkable account of the arrival of the **Prince Vijaya** from southern India sometime in the 5th century BC. His arrival is chronicled in the Mahavansa, and relates how Prince Vijaya, having been expelled by his father, landed and conquered the three indigenous tribes. This account forms the basis of Sinhalese tradition and understanding of the Sinhalese people's roots in the island. The Sinhalese language has features in common with those of northern India, whilst the language of the Tamils, the other major ethnic group in Sri Lanka, is related closely to the Dravidian languages of southern India. This ethnic difference has created a divide amongst the peoples of Sri Lanka which continues to cause major problems to this day. Firmer historical data begins to appear around the 3rd century BC, when the Maurya Empire of India embraced Sri Lanka, bringing with it the Buddhist faith that remains a distinguishing feature of the nation's culture some 2300 years on. It was during the Mauryan era, too, that Europe first heard of Sri Lanka, when rumour of a land rich in gems and spices reached the ears of Megasthenes, Alexander the Great's envoy to the Mauryan court.

A Golden Age

Sinhalese tradition states that the third king of the Vijaya dynasty, **Pandukhabhaya**, founded the city of Anuradhapura which was to be the seat of government for over a thousand years. The remains of this remarkable city were rediscovered by the British in the 19th century, and comprise the evidence of the scale and complexity of the early civilizations that existed in Asia. This is the city where, according to Buddhist legend, a sapling of the bo-tree under which the Buddha achieved enlightenment was planted. Anuradhapura was eventually abandoned as the capital in the 11th century as a result of its northern location, which made it vulnerable to frequent raids and invasions from southern India. King Vijayabahu I chose Polonnaruwa, further to the southeast, as his new capital precisely because it was further away from India and less vulnerable to attack.

Both Anuradhapura and Polonnaruwa relied on a sophisticated artificial irrigation system of canals and large man-made reservoirs or 'tanks'. Constant feuding and even foreign adventures such as that of King Parakramabahu I, (1153–86), who attacked Burma, led to the decay of the irrigation system and eventually to the abandonment of Polonnaruwa. There then followed a prolonged period of confusion, as rival Sinhalese rulers fought each other and various intruders. These internal conflicts made the island easy prey for invaders. In 1247 and again in 1258 the island was raided by Malay pirate sultans, and in 1411 the Chinese admiral Chen Ho abducted a local king. Internal divisions and factional dynastic quarrels meant that by the early 16th century the island was divided into three kingdoms: a Tamil kingdom in the north, with the Sinhalese kingdoms of Kandy in the centre and Kotte in the south and along the coastline. Then in 1505 a storm blew into Colombo a Portuguese fleet.

ADVENT OF BUDDHISM

Buddhism arrived in Sri Lanka in the 2nd century BC, and is the **religion** followed by the majority of the **Sinhalese** population. The Tamils in the north and east of the country are Hindus, as are the Tamils of southern India, with whom the Tamils of Sri Lanka have a close cultural affinity. Buddhism as a religion was largely forced out of India by resurgent Hinduism in the 3rd century BC, but survived in Lanka, which today is one of a handful of countries – including Burma, Cambodia, Thailand and Tibet – where it is the majority faith.

Below: *The sacred bo-tree at Anuradhapura is said to be the oldest tree in the world.*

THE CHINESE

In 1405, the great Chinese navigator **Chen Ho** arrived in Sri Lanka on a voyage that ultimately took him as far as Africa. Foolishly, the Sinhalese ruler Vijayabahu IV tried to kidnap Chen Ho. He failed, and paid the price six years later when the Chinese returned in force, captured the king and took him in chains to Peking. The Chinese made one of his rivals, Sri Parakrama Bahu VI, king in his place. From 1434–48 Sri Lanka paid tribute to China, but by the end of the 15th century the Chinese had lost interest in their overseas possession and the link was broken.

Opposite: *The gates and walls which surround the port of Galle date from the Dutch colonial era.*
Below: *Fishermen on the 'Parakrama Sea', built during the 12th century* AD.

The Portuguese

Portugal in the late 15th and early 16th centuries was an aggressively expanding power. **Vasco da Gama** had rounded the Cape of Good Hope in 1498 and reached India. The fleet that came to Sri Lanka in 1505 was a follow-up to that voyage. What the Portuguese were seeking was access to the spices of the east.

The Portuguese tapped into the sophisticated trade networks that existed, and became inextricably involved in local politics and power struggles. They first traded with, then assisted the Kings of Kotte in their struggles with their neighbours, and then ended up controlling Kotte. The most profitable trade was in spice, mainly in the form of cinnamon, and later ginger, nutmeg and pepper.

The Portuguese also came with a mission to spread the Roman Catholic faith. Religion could also be used as a means of control, and the Portuguese success in converting Prince Dharmapala in 1557 meant that he was little more than a Portuguese puppet. By an agreement in 1543 the Portuguese were confirmed in their control of Kotte and the coast, and guaranteed the defence of Sri Lanka in return for a tribute of cinnamon, but they never controlled the interior of the island, and their control of the coast ended in 1658 when they were ousted by the Dutch.

The Dutch

The foundation in 1600 of the Dutch East India Company, or VOC, had been designed to wrest control of far eastern markets from the hands of the Dutch Republic's enemies, Spain and Portugal. The Dutch enlisted local allies, in particular the Kingdom of Kandy, but like the Portuguese they never controlled the whole of the island. Kandy, in the inaccessible, mountainous and

heavily forested interior, was able to maintain its independence. Like the Portuguese the Dutch were attracted by the spice trade, and the island was also an important staging point on the VOC's trade routes to the East Indies, China and Japan. When the Dutch Republic declined at the end of the 18th century, its possessions overseas became natural targets for Britain, which seized the island in 1796, renaming it **Ceylon**.

British Rule

The Congress of Vienna (1815) confirmed the British in possession of Sri Lanka, and they turned their attention to conquering Kandy. They built military roads to make the inland kingdom accessible, and Kandy was quickly conquered, ending more than 2000 years of independence. A revolt in 1818 was suppressed with great severity, burning fields and villages, and some districts took decades to recover. As in India, the British set out to change the nature of the country over which they were ruling. Slavery, for example, was abolished.

In 1833 a series of reforms introduced an element of Sinhalese participation in the government, with the aim of regenerating Sri Lankan society along European lines. The main thrust though was economic liberation, which

---

THE PORTUGUESE

The Portuguese came to Sri Lanka in 1505 almost by chance, when a fleet of nine caravels en route to India was carried off course and made landfall off Colombo.
The Sinhalese were both admiring and fearful of these fair-skinned intruders in their steel armour who 'eat white stone (bread) and drink blood (wine)' and have 'guns with a noise louder than thunder'. The Portuguese had known – from the reports of **Marco Polo** and other travellers and traders – of the existence of India and Sri Lanka even before they had left Europe. They soon recognized the **strategic importance** of the island, which was an integral part of the **flourishing trade** that existed within and along the coasts of Asia.

Above: *Sri Lanka's high-lands produce some of the world's finest teas, which are picked by hand.*

COFFEE

The British introduced coffee-growing to Sri Lanka in 1824, hoping for a more lucrative crop to replace cinnamon. By the 1840s coffee was king, with hundreds of thousands of acres of forest in the Kandyan highlands cleared to make way for plantations. But in 1869 disaster struck in the shape of 'coffee rust' (*Hemileia vastratrix*) which over the next 20 years laid the plantations to waste. Many of the European planters and Sinhalese involved in coffee-growing were ruined.

---

was followed by the introduction of coffee-growing on large plantations. To work these large plantations labour was required, and the Sinhalese were unwilling to work for the low wages offered. The solution was the importation of Indian Tamils, ethnically related to the Tamils already present in Sri Lanka, but from southern India. This immigration was to cause problems later, especially in the post-independence period. Coffee failed as a crop in the 1870s due to a leaf blight, and production was switched to tea. Rubber was also an imported product that was cultivated on the island, and started by the British. Few Britons actually settled in Sri Lanka, and when nationalist stirrings did start, it was not possible for Britain to retain control indefinitely.

The British response to riots and disturbances in 1915 was repression, followed by concessions to nationalist demands. In 1919 the creation of the **Ceylon National Congress** united previous Sinhalese and Tamil organizations agitating for greater involvement in government. Pressure for change came mainly from those who had received a western education, but who also felt threatened on religious and cultural grounds by the British domination of the country. A new constitution which took account of those demands was implemented in 1920, and then amended in 1924. That response was developed in 1931 with further constitutional changes which created a universal franchise and the inclusion of Sinhalese and Tamils in government. There was little opposition to the British during WWII, and the nationalist cause was rewarded by the 1945 Soulbury Commission which drew up a constitution based on the Westminster model, and would confer independence. Elections were held at the end of 1947, and the country was **granted independence** on **4 February 1948**.

Post-Independence

The elections of 1947 were won by the United National Party (UNP) led by Don Stephen Senanayake. The UNP included representatives of all groupings, but was dominated by the western educated elite and was seen as unresponsive to the needs of the bulk of the population. In the 1956 elections the UNP was ousted by the Sri Lanka Freedom Party (SLFP), a group of nationalists with leftist leanings that pandered to Sinhalese nationalism, and Sinhala was recognized as the sole official language. This dismayed the Tamil minority and, along with moves to deport the Indian Tamil section of the population back to India, this was the start of the troubles that have bedevilled Sri Lanka in the last few decades.

A new constitution came in 1972, and the country was re-named to its present name of Sri Lanka. Buddhism was afforded

> **INDEPENDENCE DAY**
>
> Sri Lankan Independence Day (**4 February**) commemorates the granting of independence from British rule and the end of some **four centuries** of **colonialism** with colourful parades and pageants celebrating Sri Lanka's achievements as an independent nation. The day is celebrated nationwide, but the main events are held in Colombo.

Below: *The milky sap of the rubber tree is still an important foreign currency earner.*

the foremost place within the country, and Sinhala was again confirmed as the official language of government. In 1977 the UNP came into power again and changed the constitution away from the old British-based model to one that had an executive president in charge. Junius Richard Jayewardene was elected as the first president.

The 1980s saw the start of the violence that has continued on and off ever since between the Tamil and Sinhalese sections of the community. In 1983 there was violent anti-Tamil rioting, especially in Colombo. Armed Tamil resistance developed, utilizing bases in southern India among the Tamil communities there and spearheaded by the **Liberation Tigers of Tamil Eelam** (LTTE), and demands grew for complete autonomy or a Tamil state. The violence escalated and, after tortuous negotiations, in 1987 Sri Lanka and India agreed to the deployment of an **Indian Peace Keeping Force** (IPKF) to the north of the country where the Tamil areas were, to try to defuse the conflict. The Indians stayed until 1990, when the anti-insurgency task was taken over by the Sri Lankan military.

The violent nature of the conflict has continued. In October 1997 President Chandrika Bandaranaike Kumaratunga announced a power-sharing initiative aimed at ending the conflict, in which more than 50,000 have died in 25 years of civil strife. The Tamil-dominated northern and eastern regions would gain extensive autonomy. The LTTE's response was a huge bomb blast in

Colombo, killing 15 and injuring more than 100, including some 30 foreign tourists.

The LTTE has not to date deliberately targeted tourists or the tourism industry, and the main beach resort areas are relatively remote from the conflict. However, the extreme north of the country and much of the east coast, particularly the area around Batticaloa and southward, remain no-go areas for visitors at the time of writing and travel advice from the British Foreign Office, the US State Department and other governments is that visitors should avoid this part of the island. Check the latest advisories from your government before visiting Sri Lanka.

Opposite: *Sri Lanka's Muslim and Hindu minorities are represented by the green and saffron stripes on the left side of the national flag. There are bo-leaves in each corner.*

HISTORICAL CALENDAR

1,750,000 years ago Earliest archaeological artefacts found, described as Old Stone Age or Palaeolithic.

5000 years ago New Stone Age marks transformation to a settled way of life involving cultivation.

5th Century BC According to Sinhalese legend the arrival of Prince Vijaya at Puttolom; arrival of the first Aryan-Indian settlers from India.

2nd Century BC Arrival of Buddhism.

AD65 Fall of Vijaya dynasty, and takeover by Lambakannas rulers who controlled the island for the next four centuries.

1283 King Bhuvanaika Buhu I sends an emissary to the Sultan of Egypt.

14th Century Division of the island into Sinhalese kingdoms in south and centre, and Tamil kingdoms in north and east.

1505 Arrival of the Portuguese.

1543 Consolidation of Portuguese power with treaty between King Bhuvanaika Bahu and Portugal confirming Portuguese possessions and privileges.

1658 Dutch seize control of the island from Portugal.

1796 Britain ousts the Dutch.

1815 Fall of Kandyan kingdom.

1919 Formation of Ceylon National Congress.

1920 Granting of new constitution by British. Modified in 1924 to take account of nationalist aspirations.

1931 Constitution changed again to allow creation of a State Council, a universal franchise, and an element of Ceylonese participation in government.

1945 Soulbury Commission drafts constitution for the independent state of Ceylon, based largely on Westminster model.

1948, 4 February Independence from Britain as Commonwealth member.

1947 Elections won by United National Party (UNP), led by Don Stephen Senanayake, who became the first prime minister of Ceylon. UNP as a party dominated by western educated elite.

1956 Defeat of UNP, Sri Lanka Freedom Party (SLFP) takes over. Promotes a version of nationalism allied with socialism, and is led by S W R D Bandaranaike.

1959 Assassination of Bandaranaike, succeeded by his widow Sirimavo Bandaranaike.

1965 Re-election of the UNP led by the son of the first prime minister, Dudley Shelton Senanayake, in response to the instability of the SLFP administration.

1970 Return of the SLFP and Sirimara Bandaranaike as prime minister.

1972 Change of country's name from Ceylon to present-day Republic of Sri Lanka.

1972 New constitution, Sinhala confirmed as the official language.

1977 SLFP defeated and UNP takes office under Junius Richard Jayewardene. Change of constitution again to one based on French model with executive president.

1983 Series of anti-Tamil riots especially in Colombo.

1987 Deal brokered between governments of Sri Lanka and India to put an Indian Peace Keeping Force (IPKF) into the north. Tamil separatists, especially the Liberation Tigers of Tamil Eelam (LTTE), fall out with the Indian forces and fighting resumes.

1989 Jayewardene retires and is succeeded by Ranasinghe Premadasa, who had been the prime minister and was also from the UNP.

1990 Negotiated withdrawal of the IPKF, and the taking over of the anti-insurgency campaign led by the Sri Lankan military forces.

1993 Assassination of Ranasinghe Premadasa, allegedly by a Tamil extremist.

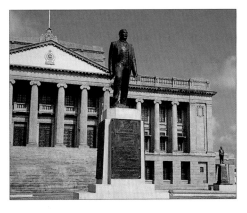

GOVERNMENT AND ECONOMY

Declared a republic in 1972, 14 years after independence, Sri Lanka has opted to stay within the **British Commonwealth** and maintains close links with Britain and with other Commonwealth member countries, especially those in Asia. The president, the prime minister and the single-house parliament are elected for a six-year term. With the power to dissolve parliament and appoint or dismiss cabinet ministers and the prime minister, the president is the real head of state, not merely a ceremonial leader.

Economic Development

Under British rule, Sri Lanka was assigned a typically colonial role as a supplier of raw materials and commodities to the imperial market. Its most important exports were rubber, coconut products and tea. Since independence, the government has aimed to diversify and modernize the economy, though these commodities (especially tea) remain important foreign currency earners. Left-leaning governments from independence until the late 1970s placed their faith in a centrally planned economy, but more economically liberal governments since the early 1980s have aimed to create a more welcoming climate for international investment and the private sector.

Trade and Industry

A comparatively well-educated workforce (with a literacy rate of around 90 per cent), coupled with low wages and the introduction of free trade zones (into which raw materials may be imported and manufactured goods exported free of tax), have made textiles and garment-making into the country's largest foreign currency

---

THE BANDARANAIKE FAMILY

In 1925, Solomon West Ridgeway Dias Bandaranaike, Oxford-educated son of a wealthy Christian landowner, rejected his father's Christian and pro-British sympathies to form the Sinhalese Popular Congress, which later merged into the United National Party. Deserting the UNP in 1951, he formed the Sri Lanka Freedom Party. The party's pro-Sinhalese Buddhist, anti-Tamil sectarianism swept it to power in 1956. S W R D Bandaranaike was assassinated by a Buddhist monk in 1959. His widow, Sirimavo Bandaranaike, took over the Freedom Party and was in and out of power through the 1960s and 1970s. She was ousted in 1977, but in 1994 her daughter, Chandrika Bandaranaike Kumaratunya, became leader of the party and was elected as the country's first female president. She appointed her mother as prime minister.

earner, accounting for 43 per cent of exports by value and pushing tea into second place. Tea now accounts for only 15 per cent of exports, while rubber accounts for 3 per cent and coconut products 2 per cent. Precious stones account for some 6 per cent of exports.

The continuing conflict between the government and the LTTE acts as a brake on economic growth and soaks up an ever-increasing chunk of government spending, with military expenditure accounting for almost 20 per cent of the budget. Gross domestic product, at Rs 771 million in 1996, shows growth of 3.8 per cent, while GNP at Rs 760 million in 1996 showed growth of 3.3 per cent. Relatively low rates of ownership of consumer durables indicate, however, that Sri Lanka is still very much a developing economy – there is only one radio for every five people, one TV for every 11 people, and around 1.4 million vehicles for a population of around 19 million. With an annual average per capita income of less than US$500, and high unemployment, at more than 12 per cent, this is hardly surprising.

Sri Lanka in the 1980s and 1990s developed an unsavoury reputation for sex tourism, with paedophiles from Europe visiting the island seeking commercial sex with under-age children. The government and the tourist industry in Sri Lanka, and its main market countries, are determined to stamp this trade out with new legislation which makes it easier to prosecute and punish offenders in their home countries or in Sri Lanka. In an attempt to encourage tourism growth, the government in 1998 announced plans for the creation of a tourism development fund with the aim to address the country's image problems.

TEA

The first tea was planted in Sri Lanka at the **Royal Botanical Gardens** in Peradeniya in 1824, but tea-growing did not become important until the late 1860s, when it was given impetus by the failure of the coffee crop. By the end of the 19th century, the island was exporting almost 68 million kilograms (150 million pounds) of tea annually. Today, about 202,347ha (500,000 acres) of land in the highlands are devoted to growing what is recognized as some of the world's finest tea.

Opposite: *The House of Assembly, Sri Lanka's Parliament building, stands on the seafront at Colombo.*

Below: *Three-wheelers like this one are the cheapest way of getting around Colombo and other towns.*

THE ANNIALATO

The people who call them-
selves Annialato and are
known rather disparagingly
by the Sinhalese as **Veddahs**
('primitive people') are the
aboriginal inhabitants of
Sri Lanka. Only a few communities are left in the
forests of the southeast and
northwest and on the east
coast, where they practise
slash-and-burn cultivation
and fishing. Their way of life
seems doomed, with government pressure on them to
assimilate into 'modern' Sri
Lankan society, and some
villagers being driven off their
ancestral lands to make way
for conservation areas.

THE PEOPLE

Sri Lanka's population is projected to be around 19
million by 2001, with population growth of about 1.2 per
cent. With a land area of just over 62,000km^2 (23,932 sq
miles), population density, at just under 300 people per
square kilometre, is relatively high. Compared with
many developing countries, the capital, Colombo – with
a population estimated at between 800,000 and one
million – accounts for a relatively small proportion of Sri
Lanka's people. Only a handful of other cities – among
them Kandy, the resort areas of Negombo and Beruwala,
and the 'gem city' of Ratnapura – have populations of
more than 100,000. In all, no more than 2 million people
live in Sri Lanka's major cities and towns, with the
remainder scattered around the country's smaller rural
towns and villages.

Ethnic Mix

Around 72 per cent of Sri Lankans are ethnic Sinhalese,
who in turn tend to divide themselves into 'low country'
dwellers in the coastal towns and lowlands, and
'Kandyan' inhabitants of the hill country. Many
Kandyans are said by lowlanders to consider themselves
a cut above their coastal cousins, as descendants of the
Kandyans who were the last Sri Lankans to fall under
the sway of a European colonial power.

Around 13 per cent of the population are Sri Lankan
Tamils. Descendants of south Indian migrants who
began to arrive in Sri Lanka as long as 2000 years ago,
crossing the narrow Palk Strait between Sri Lanka and
what is now the Indian state of Tamil Nadu, their heartland is in the north and east of the country, around
Jaffna in the extreme north, the port of Trincomalee, and
Batticaloa on the east coast. Since the mid-1970s,
demands by some Tamils for an independent state in this
part of the island have escalated into a full-scale civil war
that by 1999 had claimed up to 50,000 lives and driven
up to 700,000 people from their homes.

A further 6 per cent of the population are 'Indian'
Tamils, descendants of labourers imported by the British

Below: *Despite economic
advances, many Sri
Lankans still live off
the land, or the sea, like
this boy does.*

to work in the tea plantations of the hill country in the 19th century – employment which the proud Kandyans of the region, still smarting from their conquest by Britain, refused to consider. Though they have been the victims in the past of language discrimination and out-bursts of ethnic violence, the hill-country Tamils have mainly stayed uninvolved with the conflict in the north and east.

Sri Lankans of Arab descent, locally known as 'Moors' – though their ancestors may have arrived from the Gulf states as much as 1000 years ago – and 'Malays', descended from workers imported from the East Indies by the Dutch and the British, account for around 8 per cent of the population, and the 'Burgher' community, the Christian descendants of Portuguese and Dutch settlers who intermarried with the Sinhalese, account for a tiny minority of less than 1 per cent, most of them resident in Colombo and Galle.

Regardless of the country's colonial past and its present-day troubles, Sri Lankans of all ethnic groups are generally extremely friendly, helpful and welcoming to visitors in their country.

Above: *Colourful Tamil tea pickers, in the rain.*

THE BURGHERS

Sri Lanka's tiny Burgher com-munity, descended from Dutch and Portuguese colo-nialists, played a major part in running the country under British rule, when they formed an educated, English-speaking class which dominated the administration and the professions. After independence, however, their position was eroded as successive governments promoted Sinhalese as the national language, and Burghers were treated with some suspicion. Many have emigrated to the UK and to Australia, and there are now probably fewer than 15,000 people of Burgher descent in Sri Lanka.

Above: *Betel nut, a mild stimulant, is favoured by many Sri Lankans, and stains teeth and gums bright crimson.*

Language

Language has been a contentious issue in Sri Lanka. In the 1970s, Sinhalese demagogues promoted efforts to make Sinhala – the language of the Sinhalese majority – the sole language of education, administration and government. This was perceived by the Tamil minority as a deliberate move to keep Tamils out of government and exclude them from further education, and was a major cause of the discontent that eventually erupted into inter-communal violence. Subsequently, a compromise was reached in an attempt to satisfy both the disgruntled Tamil community and hard-line Sinhalese nationalists. **Tamil** and **Sinhala** are ranked equally as 'official' languages, while Sinhala is the 'national' language. Tamil – which is also the largest language group in southern India and the main language of Tamil Nadu, the Indian state closest to Sri Lanka – is the mother tongue of about 20 per cent of the population in total, including both northern and hill-country 'Indian' Tamil communities, while Sinhala is the first language of the Sinhalese majority and of most Sri Lankans of Malay and Arab descent.

Meanwhile, **English** is still almost universally spoken by educated people of all communities, and is the language with which Sri Lanka communicates with the outside world. Despite being the language of the former colonial power, English is also politically neutral. Most of the people you are likely to encounter in shops, hotels, restaurants and when travelling on public transport are likely to speak enough English for you to get by. Taxi drivers usually speak some English, and bus and railway personnel are usually quite fluent. Out in the countryside, English may be less widely spoken, though it is rare to find yourself completely unable to communicate.

Religion

Sri Lanka's majority religion is the austere Theravada ('small vehicle') school of Buddhism, imported from India during the 3rd century BC and followed today by the vast majority of the Sinhalese ethnic group.

In 1972 **Buddhism** was made virtually a national religion, and acknowledged by the government as the country's paramount faith, a move which disturbed Tamil Hindus and members of other faiths. **Hinduism**, an even older religion, is the faith of the Tamil minority, while there are significant **Muslim** and **Christian** minorities which each account for between 7 and 8 per cent of the population. The Christian community comprises descendants of the early Portuguese and Dutch colonists who intermarried with local communities, as well as converts from both the Sinhalese Buddhist and Tamil Hindu communities. The Muslim community also includes Sinhalese and Tamil converts, but its numbers are bolstered by the descendants of Arab traders from the Gulf, who arrived as early as the 7th century AD, and by people of Malay descent, whose ancestors were imported from the East Indies as labourers by the Dutch and later by the British.

There is a certain amount of overlap between faiths, with Christians and Muslims praying alongside Hindus and Buddhists at some holy places, such as Kataragama in the southeast and Adams Peak in the highlands.

Hinduism, the faith of Sri Lanka's Tamil minority, is the oldest and most complex faith in the world. Born in the Indus Valley with the Indian sub-continent's first civilization, its pantheon was added to by Aryan

> **THE EIGHT-FOLD PATH**
>
> The Buddha taught that all life is suffering; that this suffering comes from selfish desire; that eliminating selfish desire from one's life is the way to escape suffering; and that the Buddhist 'eight-fold path' or 'middle may' is the way to achieve this. The 'eight rights' which make up the eight-fold path are right understanding, right thought, right speech, right action, right aspiration, right exertion, right attentiveness and right concentration.

Below: *Images of the Buddha are revered by Sri Lanka's Buddhist majority and are found all over the island.*

HINDUISM

With its dozens of deities, many of whom have several different personalities, Hinduism baffles the outsider. There are three major deities: **Brahma**, the creator; **Vishnu**, the preserver; and **Shiva**, who represents destruction and rebirth. All-seeing Brahma, the most remote of the gods from humankind, is depicted with four faces, often accompanied by his consort, the goddess Sarasvati. Shiva is represented by the stone lingam, a stylized penis symbolizing virility and male fertility. Vishnu is the most human of the three great Hindu gods, appearing in a series of incarnations which symbolize the nine ages of the world. In his first six incarnations he appeared in the form of a wild boar or a manticore (half-man, half-lion), but in his seventh he appeared as King Rama, leader of mankind and the gods against Ravana, the demon-king of Lanka in Hinduism's most accessible epic, the *Ramayana*. Hinduism also has a large supporting cast of lesser deities, like Rama's faithful ally Hanuman, king of the monkeys; and Ganesha, elephant-headed son of Shiva and his consort Parvati, and god of wisdom and wealth.

Right: *Hindu temples, like this one in Negombo, are brilliantly colourful and covered in statues of gods and goddesses.*

invaders who started to arrive in India from the north in around 1500BC.

Buddhism, the faith of Sri Lanka's Sinhalese majority, grew from Hinduism and retains some of the elements of the Hindu religion, such as a belief in reincarnation. Unlike Hinduism – and uniquely among the world's great faiths – Buddhism has no gods, and in that sense is a philosophy and a code of conduct rather than a religion as such.

Buddhism began some 2500 years ago with the teachings of Siddartha Gautama, prince of a north Indian Hindu dynasty, who gave up his earthly power and wealth in achieving enlightenment.

Bhuddhism's greatest convert was the Mauryan Emperor Ashok, whose realm at its most powerful comprised almost all the subcontinent (except for the far

south), and who sent his son
Mahindra to carry the Buddha's
teachings to the Lankan kings of
Anuradhapura. There, it found an
enthusiastic following, and the
Sinhalese kingdoms remained firmly
Buddhist long after Buddhism had
waned on the Indian mainland.

Christianity was brought to Sri
Lanka by the Portuguese, and the
overwhelming majority of Sri
Lanka's 900,000-strong Christian
minority still follow the Roman
Catholic faith of the first Christian
converts, with only around 120,000
adhering to other Christian churches.

Sport and Recreation

Sri Lankans have triumphed internationally at **athletics**,
among them, in the 1990s, the sprinter Susanthika
Jayasinghe (tipped as a potential gold medallist in the
2000 Olympic Games in Sydney) and others, including
Sriyani Kulawansa and Sugath Tillekeratne. But it is
cricket that is the first and truest love of all Sri Lankan
sport fans. When Sri Lanka, led by Arjuna Ranatunga,

Above: *St Anthony's
Church in the Sri Lankan
capital is one of the island's
oldest. Christianity arrived
with the Portuguese.*
Below: *Colombo's Galle
Face Green is a popular
spot for a game of cricket.*

trounced the giants of
world cricket to win the
1996 Wills Trophy in one-
day internationals, there
was dancing in the streets,
and when Sri Lanka's
team is playing in major
international events it is
with the whole island
watching or listening.
Players are major stars,
and probably the most
popular public figures in
the country. Any patch of
relatively flat wasteland

or village square is likely to have its complement of small boys playing an improvised game, and no matter how crude or aged the equipment, the players will be as deadly serious as any world cup final team. If you are a cricket fan, you may want to watch a game at the Kettarama Stadium in north Colombo or at Asgiriya, in Kandy, where cricket is played from January to April.

Sri Lanka also abounds in **watersports**, with some excellent scuba diving from qualified dive shops at major resorts, and windsurfing and sailing equipment for hire at all main beach resort areas. These, however, are sports intended primarily for visiting holiday-makers, though some Sri Lankans have taken them up too.

Above: *Elaborate masks evoke demons and deities and are popular souvenirs to take home.*

GRATIAEN MEMORIAL PRIZE

Michael Ondaatje's international success has enabled him to establish the Gratiaen Memorial Prize. This is for works in English by Sri Lankan authors and has been won in recent years by Carl Muller (1993), for *The Jam Fruit Tree*, first in a trilogy of works about a Colombo Burgher dynasty.

THE ARTS

Sri Lankan visual arts, architecture, literature, music and dance all bear the stamp of the country's centuries-old Buddhist culture. Poetry, as well as music and dance, were almost entirely ceremonial and devotional until well after the fall of the Kandyan kingdom to the British, but by the mid-19th century Sri Lanka was being opened up to outside cultural influences by the advent of the printing press. However, a strongly conservative Buddhist tradition has not provided fertile ground for vernacular literature to grow in. The fierce political repression which followed the leftist revolts of 1971 and 1987–88 and the ethnic troubles of the 1980s and 1990s have also made it hard for writers to write freely. That said, Sri Lanka has its share of home-grown literary talent. Probably the best known of its authors is Michael Ondaatje, author of the acclaimed novel, *The English Patient*, which is also a popular screen picture.

Music and Dance

Music and dance in Sri Lanka are still closely tied up with religious ritual. Kandyan or 'high country' dance has evolved from village dances performed to appeal to local deities, and is accompanied by the complex rhythms of several drummers who use a percussion instrument called the *gatebere* – a wooden drum with leather heads of monkey skin at one end and cowhide at the other, which make contrasting tones.

Dancers, usually women, go through a routine of sinuous poses and flowing arm movements. 'Low country' or 'devil-mask' dancing is also accompanied by drummers, who use a special 'demon drum' to enhance the steps and movements of dancers wearing the grotesque masks which represent the 18 demons of disease. These dances were – and sometimes still are – performed with the intention of persuading the demon to leave the afflicted person.

FRESCOES AND SCULPTURES

Common themes of Buddhist temple friezes and murals include **Maya's dream**, in which the Buddha's mother saw a white elephant, portending his birth. The **Buddha's birth** is also frequently depicted, as are scenes in which he first sees the cruelties of life outside the privileged world of the royal palace, and leaves the palace for a life of ascetic contemplation, before finally becoming liberated from the cycle of birth and rebirth in the scene called **Mahaparinirvana**.

Art and Architecture

The most prominent examples of Sri Lanka's Buddhist-influenced architectural heritage are the dagobas which can be seen from one end of the country to the other. In the shape of a dome, the dagoba, usually painted white, often enshrines a relic of the Buddha, such as a hair or a tooth, and is usually massively constructed of brick covered with a coat of plaster.

The pantiled roofs and verandahs which grace many older buildings are the legacy of the Portuguese and Dutch. Galle has many fine old Dutch buildings, while in Kandy and Nuwara Eliya there are many surviving buildings from the British colonial era which would not look out of place in an English country town.

Below: *The massive sea-facing ramparts of Galle failed to protect the Dutch garrison from English conquest.*

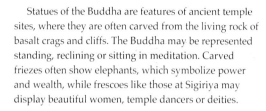

SEAFOOD

Among the delights of Sri Lankan cooking for the tourist are many kinds of fish and other seafood, from tasty, firm-fleshed deep-sea fish like tuna to lobster, prawn and crab found in abundance in the lagoons and coastal shallows. Smaller fish are often preserved by drying, and Sri Lanka imports tons of dried fish from the tiny Indian Ocean islands of the Maldives archipelago, several hundred miles to the northwest. Strong tasting and strong smelling, these are a local delicacy, but are very much an acquired taste. Squid, cuttlefish and octopus all also make an appearance on the menu, grilled or served in curry.

Statues of the Buddha are features of ancient temple sites, where they are often carved from the living rock of basalt crags and cliffs. The Buddha may be represented standing, reclining or sitting in meditation. Carved friezes often show elephants, which symbolize power and wealth, while frescoes like those at Sigiriya may display beautiful women, temple dancers or deities.

FOOD AND DRINK

Sri Lanka is blessed with fertile soil, rich seas and a tropical climate in which delicious fruit, fresh vegetables and flavoursome spices grow abundantly. That abundance is reflected in the country's cooking, which also shows the influences of the many races who have settled the island of Sri Lanka in past centuries.

Rice and Curry

No traditional meal in Sri Lanka is complete without rice, usually served plainly boiled or steamed and accompanied by any of dozens of different curry dishes.

Usually, a main meal comprises one central curry dish – chicken, lamb, beef, fish or prawn – with a selection of vegetable and *dhal* (lentil) dishes. Along with these are side dishes of chutney and pickle. Some of these are cooling (such as mango chutney), while others are fiery. Among the spiciest of all Sri Lankan side dishes is *sambol*, a potent paste blended from onion, coconut, chilli, lime juice and dried fish and served with rice. Coconut milk is a major ingredient in all Sri Lankan curries, which are generally lighter and less rich than the curry dishes of northern India, and have much in common with the cooking of the Indian south.

Many Sri Lankans, both Hindu and Buddhist, follow a vegetarian diet at least part of the time, and Sri Lanka is an excellent destination for vegetarians, with many delicious meat-free dishes to choose from on the menu.

Left: *Cinnamon, cumin, cardamom, nutmeg, pepper and ginger are among the spices grown in Sri Lanka.*
Opposite: *The silvery catch of the famous stilt-fishermen of Sri Lanka's south coast.*

Spices

The spices which first drew Europeans to the island – cloves, cardamom, nutmeg, cinnamon and pepper – still grow in great abundance in Sri Lanka. They lend richness and zest to many dishes, often in proportions that depend on availability and the chef's personal taste rather than on any fixed recipe.

Drink

Fruit juices are widely available but should be treated with caution as they may not have been blended with water that is safe to drink. Tap water may be contaminated, particularly during the monsoon season. You should be able to trust fruit juices in main resort hotels, but those sold in smaller restaurants and roadside stands are best avoided. Bottled water and soft drinks are widely available.

Grapes are among the few fruits that will not grow in Sri Lanka, so all wines are imported and are therefore relatively expensive and often of indifferent quality. Lion lager, the country's main brand of beer, is relatively expensive in Sri Lankan terms, but like almost everything else in Sri Lanka is cheap by international standards. Imported beers, and Guinness stout brewed under licence, are also available in bars and restaurants in the main tourist areas.

FOREIGN FOOD

Colonial dishes which have stood the test of time include *lampreis* – curried rice with meatballs, baked in a banana leaf – which was introduced by the Dutch from the East Indies. British-style roast beef still sometimes appears on the menu, but it is the new empire of tourism that is having the most profound effect on Sri Lankan eateries with Italian, French, and German restaurants appearing in Colombo and in the main holiday resorts. Virtually every Sri Lankan budget restaurant also claims to serve 'Chinese' dishes – usually no more than a handful of rice and noodle dishes such as chow mein and chop suey. Many of the top-end international hotels in Colombo have Japanese, Chinese and North Indian restaurants in addition to their Sri Lankan and international eating places.

2
Colombo

Colombo, Sri Lanka's bustling capital, is located on the country's west coast and with a population of between 800,000 and one million (estimates vary) is by far the country's biggest city, as well as its window on the world. Its natural harbour at the mouth of the Kelani River was a magnet for successive traders and conquerors – first Arab merchants, then Portuguese, Dutch and British imperialists.

The city is a sometimes jarring mix of old and new, with a central cluster of high-rise office blocks and hotels overshadowing red-tiled colonial-era buildings and sprawling street markets which overflow with high-piled fruit and vegetables, colourful silks and cottons, and deliciously fragrant spices.

On its crowded streets stand places of worship symbolic of Sri Lanka's multi-ethnic heritage: graceful Buddhist *viharas*, for instance, stand close to gaudy temples encrusted with Hindu statuary, and Muslim mosques with slender minarets.

Colombo's streets, which buzz with life during the day – when its population is swollen by some 400,000 commuting workers – are virtually empty after nightfall, with little nightlife outside a handful of international-standard hotels.

During the day, however, its colourful street markets, colonial-era buildings, museums and galleries, churches, mosques and temples, and the lovely Viharamahadevi Park with it beautiful trees, make it a great place to explore on foot.

DON'T MISS

** **Pettah:** bazaar district packed with shops and stalls.
** **National Museum and Puppetry and Children's Museum:** exhibits give insights into life in ancient and modern Sri Lanka.
** **Dutch Period Museum:** glimpse into the vanished era of the Dutch occupation.
* **Viharamahadevi Park:** Colombo's largest and most elegant green space.

Opposite: *The Clock Tower, in Colombo's downtown Fort district.*

Originally named **Kolomtota**, Colombo was the main seaport of Kotte, the country's 15th- and 16th-century capital. Known to Arab traders as Kalamba, the city attracted the rapacious Portuguese as early as 1505 and became the bastion of their rule for almost 150 years. Surprisingly little remains to attest to this era, apart from a scattering of Portuguese surnames in the telephone directory and a handful of Roman Catholic churches and seminaries. Nor are there many mementoes of the Dutch who expelled the Portuguese in the mid-17th century. The central area of the city is still known as **Fort**, but the remnants of the colonial battlements have long since been demolished, or incorporated in newer buildings.

There are more mementoes of the British period, including the neo-Classical old parliament building, the Victorian-era **President's House** (still often called 'Queen's House'), and the grandly mercantile brick façade of **Cargill's**, a splendid 19th-century department store that has changed little since the 19th-century heyday of Sri Lanka's British tea planters.

FORT

Fort, between Colombo Harbour to the north and the murky urban lagoon of Beira Lake to the south, is the heart of Colombo. The Portuguese built and extended their fortress here during more than a century of conquest and resistance. It was taken over by the Dutch, and finally demolished by the British after they completed their conquest of the country in the mid-19th century. Today, the area is the city's financial and commercial heart and houses Colombo's main international hotels, as well as Sri Lanka's seat of government.

The mid-19th-century **Clock Tower**, at the corner of Janadihipathi Mawatha and Chatham Street, was originally a lighthouse and is now a handy landmark for the city centre area. Other landmarks include the **President's House** and **Presidential Gardens**, a palatial neo-Classical building which was originally the home of the British Governors and is now the residence of Sri Lanka's president; it is sadly off limits to visitors.

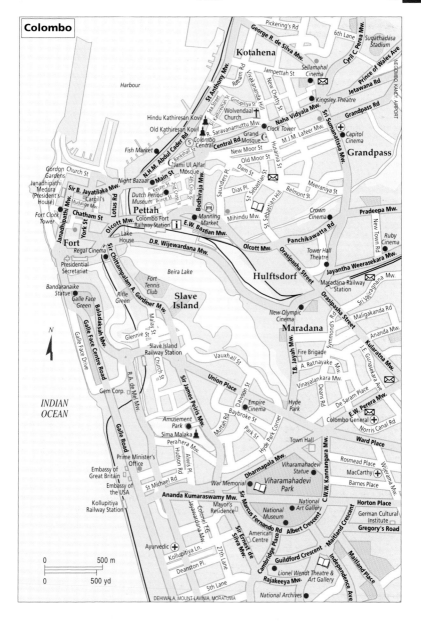

Colombo

Kotahena

Harbour

Hindu Kathiresan Kovil
Old Kathiresan Kovil

Fish Market

Gordon Church St
Gardens
Janadhipathi
Medura
(President's
House)

Fort Clock
Tower

Pettah

Night Bazaar
Dutch Period
Museum

Fort

Regal Cinema

Presidential
Secretariat

Bandaranaike
Statue
Galle Face
Green

Slave
Island

INDIAN
OCEAN

Slave Island
Railway Station

Gem Corp.

Amusement
Park
Sima Malaka

Prime Minister's
Office
Embassy of
Great Britain
Embassy of
the USA
Kollupitiya
Railway Station

Ananda Kumaraswamy Mw.

Ayurvedic

Pickering's Rd
George R. de Silva Mw.
6th Lane
Sugathadasa
Stadium

Jampettah St
Sellamahal
Cinema

Kingsley Theatre

Wolvendaal
Church
Clock Tower
Grand
Mosque

New Moor St
Old Moor St

Dam St

Saunders Pl
Dias Pl.
St. Sebastian Hill
Belmont St

Manning
Market
Mihindu Mw.

Lake
House

D.R. Wijewardana Mw.

Beira Lake

Fort
Tennis
Club
Rifle
Green

Malay St

Glennie St

Church St

Vauxhall St

Union Place

Dawson St
Empire
Cinema
Baybroke St

Park St

Hyde
Park
Hyde Park Corner

War Memorial

Mayor's
Residence
National
Museum
American
Centre

Kollupitiya Ln.
Deanston Pl.

Naha Vidyala Mw.

Sri Sumanatissa Mw.
Grandpass Rd
Capitol
Cinema

Grandpass

M.J.M. Lafeer Mw.

Hikatna St

Meeraniya St

Crown
Cinema
Pradeepa Mw.

Ruby
Cinema

New Town Rd

Panchikawatta Rd
Tower Hall
Theatre

Olcott Mw.
Orasipasha Street

Hulftsdorf

Jayantha Weerasekara Mw.
Maradana Railway
Station

Sri Vanyagaha Mw.

New Olympic
Cinema

Maradana

Orasipasha Street
Maligakanda Rd
Ananda Mw.

Kularatna Mw.

J.E. Gunasekara Ave.

Fire Brigade
A. Ratnayake Mw.

Vinayalankara Mw.

T.B. Jayah Mw.
Simmons Rd

De Saram Place
E.W. Perera Mw.
Colombo General
Norris Canal Rd

Town Hall

Ward Place

Rosmead Place
MacCarthy
Barnes Place

Dharmapala Mw.
Viharamahadevi
Statue

Viharamahadevi
Park

National
Art Gallery

C.W.W. Kannangara Mw.

Horton Place

German Cultural
Institute
Gregory's Road

Albert Crescent

Maitland Crescent

Maitland Place

Guildford Crescent

Lionel Wendt Theatre &
Art Gallery
Rajakeeya Mw.

National Archives

Independence Ave.

5th Lane
27th Lane

Sir Ernest de Silva Mw.
Sir Marcus Fernando Rd
Colonel T.G. Jayawardana Mw.

Cambridge Place

St. Anthony Mw.
Rahan Rd
Vivakananda Hill
New Chetty St

Jetawana Rd
Prince of Wales Ave

Cyril C Perera Mw.

Jami Ul Alfar
Mosque
Main St
Keyzer St
2nd Cross St
Prince St
1st Cross St
3rd Cross St

Bodhiraja Mw.

Colombo
Central
Central Rd
Gintuptiya St
R. Saravanamuttu Mw.
Bankshall St
Kathiresan St
Sea Street

Sir B. Jayatilaka Mw.
Cargill's
Mudalige Mw.
N.H.M. Abdul Cader Rd
Chatham St

Lotus Rd
York St
Olcott Mw.

Colombo Fort
Railway Station
E.W. Eastman Mw.

Sir Chittampalam A. Gardiner Mw.

Galle Face Centre Road
Baladaksah Mw.
Galle Face Drive

Galle Road

R.A. de Mel Mw.

Sir James Peiris Mw.

Murtah St
Hudson Rd
Alwis Pl
Perahera Mw.
St. Michael Rd

Janadhipathi Mw.

INDEPENDENCE Ave.

N

0   500 m
0   500 yd

DEHIWALA, MOUNT LAVINIA, MORATUWA

NEGOMBO, KANDY, AIRPORT

1. Hindu Kathiresan Kovil
2. Old Kathiresan Kovil
3. Wolvendaal Church
4. Grand Mosque
5. Jami Ul Alfar Mosque

Right *Cargill's department store in central Colombo, overlooked by the twin towers of the World Trade Centre, sells everything under the sun.*

Cargill's *

This **once grand department store** at the corner of York Street and Sir Baron Jayatilaka Mawatha, built to supply British planters and colonial administrators with every imported luxury, has changed little since its Victorian heyday, and its interior, with glass and mahogany cabinets and brasswork, is a **living mercantile museum**. It is open during usual shopping hours.

PETTAH

Immediately east of Fort (across the narrow canal that separates the outer harbour from the Beira Lake) is Pettah, a maze of streets and alleys piled and crammed with goods of every description, from colourful textiles, gold and silver, and colonial-era antiquities to the necessities of everyday life – spices, fruit and vegetables, reeking heaps of dried fish, paraffin, batteries, electrical goods, clothes and footwear. Whatever you are looking for, you'll find it in Pettah – though shopping here, which can call for determined bargaining, is not for the faint of heart. Among the most interesting streets for both sightseeing and shopping is **Sea Street**, in the northeast corner of Pettah, with its goldsmiths' workshops and the dramatically colourful **Hindu Kathiresan** and **Old Kathiresan** *kovils* (temples). These are the starting point for the Vel festival, celebrating the marriage of the god Murugan (the top Tamil deity) to his queen

---

VEL FESTIVAL

Colombo's main **Hindu festival**, celebrated by the Tamil community, is held during the **August full moon**, when the gorgeously decorated Vel chariot of Skanda, the Hindu god of war, carries his weapons around the Hindu temples of the capital. Skanda, an aspect of Shiva, also has a major temple and pilgrimage site at Kataragama, in southeast Sri Lanka, where pilgrims flock during the July/August Esala pilgrimage season.

Deivanai and concubine Valli Ammal, and held each year in August. Not too far from these stand the **Grand Mosque**, the most important mosque for Sri Lanka's Muslim population, on New Moor Street, whose very name reflects a long-standing heritage of contact with the Arab world, and the **Jami Ul Alfar Mosque**, at the corner of Bankshall Street and Second Cross Street. Built at the beginning of the 20th century, its decorative brickwork, patterned in red and white, is conspicuous.

Dutch Period Museum **

Built during the second half of the 17th century as the residence of Count August van Ranzow, the Dutch East India Company's governor in Colombo, this attractive old building at 95 Prince Street is one of the few surviving remnants of Colombo's Dutch colonial heritage. On the fringes of Pettah, it is surrounded by market stalls and antique shops. Its rather chaotic collection includes coins, weapons, pottery, portraits and furniture from the period of Dutch rule, and also traces the descent of the dwindling 'Burgher' community. Open Saturday– Thursday 09:00–17:00.

Below: *Shops and stalls in Colombo's crowded Pettah market district overflow with goods of all kinds.*

Wolvendaal Church **

Another relic of the Dutch period is this stone church on Wolvendaal Street, built in 1749. Worth looking at are the **tombstones** set into the floor, which were moved from a church within the Fort in 1813. The dates on the tombs of several Dutch governors, whose bones were reinterred here, reveal how risky life could be for the Dutch conquerors: even in peacetime, the death toll from disease was high and many died after only a short stay in Colombo. Open during usual church hours.

CINNAMON

Of all the spices that drew the Dutch to Sri Lanka, cinnamon was the most important. Not content with the piecemeal cultivation traditional to the island, they began systematically setting up plantations, and by the time they were ousted by Britain, in the late 18th century, the island had a monopoly of the world's cinnamon trade. With the British takeover, boom years followed as new markets for the spice opened up, but Britain could not keep a monopoly forever, and by the 1820s other spice-growing countries were in competition and the price of cinnamon plummeted. It is still grown, but is not economically vital.

GALLE FACE AREA

Galle Face Green, immediately south of the Fort, is a long, thin park which fills up with food stalls on weekend evenings and is a popular meeting place for local people. A narrow arm of Beira Lake separates this district from **Slave Island**, actually a peninsula where the Dutch imprisoned slaves from their Asian colonies.

Galle Road, Colombo's long seafront boulevard, runs south from Galle Face Green, eventually becoming the main coastal road to Galle and the south. It's always crowded with traffic and short on charm, but as the city's main thoroughfare it also has some of the best shopping and a number of important buildings, including the official residence of Sri Lanka's premier, the US Embassy, the British High Commission and some of the city's top hotels.

Cinnamon Gardens

The Cinnamon Gardens district, approximately a block inland (east) from Galle Road, shows not a trace of the spice plantations from which it gets its name, but is now the city's university and diplomatic quarter and its wealthiest residential area. With its boulevards lined with jacaranda and frangipani trees, it is in sharp contrast to the grime, commerce and visible poverty of the Pettah area to the north. The white-domed **Town Hall**, said to have been modelled on the US White House, is a major landmark, overlooking the semicircular expanse of **Viharamahadevi Park**, Colombo's largest and most

Right: *Colombo's Town Hall, with its colonnades and white dome, is modelled on Washington's White House, home of US presidents.*

elegant and attractive green space. The park is at its prettiest from March to May, before the monsoon arrives, when its trees and shrubberies are in brilliant flower. In the centre of the park a statue of **Queen Victoria** commemorates her rule over the island, while on the lawns near the Town Hall a golden image of the **Buddha** represents an even older heritage.

National Museum and Puppetry and Children's Museum **

At Sir Marcus Fernando Mawatha (also known as Albert Crescent), next to the Viharamahadevi Park, the **National Museum** was Sri Lanka's first and was founded in 1877. Its collection spans several centuries and a range of cultures, from the Sinhala kingdoms through to the British era. Highlights include the royal trappings of the last **Kings of Kandy**. There is also some superb stone sculpture, as well as Hindu bronzes and wooden carvings, Sri Lankan and European furniture and ceramics, and (to Western eyes) a fine array of grotesque masks representing Buddhist demons and deities. The museum's huge **library** of more than 500,000 books is primarily of interest to scholars, but some of its collection of 4000 palm leaf manuscripts – created by etching the lettering into the fibrous surface of the leaf – are on display. A small **gallery** of mid-19th-century paintings and etchings shows Sri Lanka through the eyes of British artists.

Within the National Museum, on the first floor, is the **Puppetry and Children's Museum**. Puppetry is a living part of Sri Lanka's cultural heritage, and the museum displays traditional Sri Lankan figures and marionettes from all over the world, with regular weekend performances. It is open Saturday–Thursday, 09:00–17:00.

Above: *Puppetry plays a significant role in Sri Lanka's living heritage, as seen here at the Puppetry and Children's Museum.*

OLA MANUSCRIPTS

Palm-leaf was used by the Kandyan kings and earlier rulers to record royal decrees, genealogies, histories and religious scriptures. The tough leaves were cut into strips and then inscribed by cutting letters into the green outer layer of the leaf to reveal the tough inner fibre. The dried strips were then stitched together to create a manuscript that looks like a miniature Venetian blind covered with curling characters.

Above: *The National Art Gallery and Cultural Museum is more impressive from the outside than within.*

National Art Gallery (Cultural Museum) *

At 106 Ananda Kumaraswamy Mawatha, this gallery on the edge of Viharamahadevi Park houses a rather humdrum assortment of **portraits** of Sri Lanka's independence pioneers and heads of state. The changing programme of shows by contemporary Sri Lankan artists is sometimes more interesting. Open 08:00–17:00 daily.

Natural History Museum *

Housed in the same building as the National Art Gallery, this collection is a hit and miss affair with stuffed birds and animals displayed in cases showing their natural habitat, and sections dealing with Sri Lanka's geology, climate, and plant life. The most striking display is of an **elephant's skeleton**, and there are also displays which focus on some of the country's ambitious hydro-electric and irrigation engineering schemes. Open 09:00–17:00 daily.

AROUND COLOMBO

Colombo's urban sprawl has pushed the city limits northwards in the direction of Negombo (where the city's Katunayake International Airport is located) and southwards towards Mount Lavinia. These residential suburbs and resort areas have the beaches closest to the city centre, and as a result were the first to be developed for **beach tourism**. Both areas, however, have been overtaken by more attractive resorts with better beaches in the southwest. They have also suffered from the slump in tourism caused by the civil war from the late 1980s onwards, and many of the big **resort hotels** built here in anticipation of an ongoing tourism boom are as a result somewhat under-used and very affordable.

DEHIWALA ZOO

The big deal at the Dehiwala Zoo at Allen Avenue, in the suburb of Dehiwala, 10km (6 miles) south of the city centre, is the daily **elephant show**, with a troop of trained elephants being put through their paces. Whether you enjoy this will depend on how you feel about performing animals. Open daily 08:00–18:00, elephant show 17:00 daily.

Negombo **

For a shorter beach holiday, or as a stopover on your first or last night in Sri Lanka, Negombo, 37km (23 miles) north of Colombo city centre, has the virtue of being the closest beach resort to Katunayake International Airport. For that reason, it also appears in a number of tour operator brochures. Nicknamed 'Little Rome' because of its numerous Catholic churches – a survival from the period of Portuguese rule – Negombo surrounds a **lagoon** which is rich in fish and until the advent of tourism provided most of the villagers with a living. Today, tourism provides a ready market for the lagoon's prawns and lobsters, and for deep-water fish like tuna, shark and amberjack, but the picturesque twin-hulled sailing canoes are slowly being ousted by modern wooden or plastic-hulled, motor-driven boats. Nevertheless, the narrow streets and colourful stucco churches of the old part of town make Negombo acceptably picturesque for a short stay, and there are more than a dozen luxury resort hotels to choose from.

Negombo's **beach** is less than brilliant by Sri Lankan standards – there are other, far better beaches elsewhere – and the sea is often murky as a result of silt carried into it from the 12km (7.5-mile) lagoon and the network of freshwater channels feeding into it.

> **COLOMBO WETLANDS**
>
> Only 7km (4 miles) from the airport, just off the main Colombo–Negombo road, the **Muthurajawela Marshes** are Sri Lanka's first wetlands reserve, with **boat rides** from the visitor centre through a wide expanse of marshland which connects with the Negombo Lagoon. Birds to be seen include purple herons, egrets, four kingfisher species, grebes, moorhens, lesser whistling ducks, and painted storks, while toque monkeys may also be seen from the boat. The marshlands also shelter 15 amphibian species, 37 reptile species and 34 mammal species.

Left: *Fishing boats like this outrigger vessel on the lagoon at Negombo, north of Colombo, have changed little over centuries.*

Dutch Fort *

Commanding the entrance to the lagoon, the ruined fort dates from 1678, according to the date inscribed above its stone gateway. It was built some 34 years after the Dutch wrested Sri Lanka from Portugal, and defended the natural harbour from which the Dutch East India Company exported cinnamon and other spices, which were the island's most valuable exports. Next to the walls is a Dutch cemetery. Open during daylight hours.

St Mary's Church **

This is the most picturesque of the town's many Catholic churches and chapels, testimony to the enthusiasm with which the local Karava people adopted Catholicism under Portuguese tutelage. The **painted ceiling** is well worth a look. Open during usual church hours.

Above: *St Mary's Church in Negombo dates back to the Portuguese era, and is worth a visit for its gorgeous painted ceiling.*

Mount Lavinia *

About 11km (6 miles) south of Colombo city centre, Mount Lavinia has a beach with a potentially dangerous undertow and occasionally polluted waters which diminish the appeal of its golden sands and swaying palms. Much of its reputation rests on the charm of the **Mount Lavinia Hotel**. In around 1805–6 the then British Governor, **Sir Thomas Maitland**, built an official residence here, naming it after his mistress. It was rebuilt between 1823 and 1827 by one of his successors, Edward Barnes; it became a government rest house in 1877 and was converted into a hotel in

1895. Modern additions have obliterated much of its old-world charm, despite attempts to maintain some continuity with its past. A **superb pool** with great sea views makes up for the deficiencies of the beach.

Kalutara *

This bustling village at the mouth of the Kalu Ganga, 45km (27 miles) south of Colombo, was, like Negombo, a very important

Above: *Resorts abound in shops selling traditional local crafts such as coconut fibre work, pictured here on a Colombo street.*

entrepôt for the cinnamon and nutmeg trades but is now better known for its **coconut palm gardens** and for coconut-fibre mats, rope and baskets. Kalutara also claims to have the tastiest **mangosteens** in Sri Lanka. A purple fruit with white, segmented flesh and a deliciously tart flavour, the mangosteen is said to be at its best in June.

Basket Centre *

The Basket Centre is in the middle of the village. See baskets and other wares being woven from coconut fibre, with the opportunity to buy. The tough, well-made baskets come in handy if you haven't enough space in your luggage for all your other souvenir purchases, and make good gifts too. Open 08:00–17:00 daily.

Gangatilaka Vihara *

On the banks of the Kalu Ganga, next to the road bridge, stands the Gangatilaka Vihara, a large dagoba (Buddhist shrine) beside which stands a sacred bo-tree. The hollow dagoba has an unusual **painted interior**. It is open during daylight hours. If you intend to go inside, a small cash offering, to be placed in the box fixed to the sacred tree, will be appreciated.

DURUTU PERAHERA

Peraheras, or Buddhist religious processions, are held at important temples all over Sri Lanka. The *Durutu Perahera*, held on 1 January, takes place at the **Kelaniya Temple**, 12km (8 miles) east of Colombo city centre near the suburb of Kotte, with torch bearers, drummers and brightly caparisoned Asian elephants.

Colombo at a Glance

Colombo is most pleasant from September to late April. From May to September, the **south-west monsoon** deposits heavy rain on the west coast and raises heavy seas which make swimming dangerous at Negombo and Mount Lavinia.

GETTING THERE

By air: International scheduled flights by the national carrier Air Lanka and other European carriers from Amsterdam, London, Frankfurt and other European cities, mostly via Dubai. Direct scheduled connections to Delhi, Bombay, Singapore and other Asian capitals. Air Lanka also flies to the Maldives. International flight information, tel: (01) 587912/500732 or 508040.

By rail: Trains run from Fort Railway Station in Colombo to Kandy in the central highlands, Trincomalee on the east coast, and Anuradhapura in the northeast. Fort Railway Station, information, tel: (01) 435838.

By road: Coach services oper-ate from Colombo to points throughout Sri Lanka, with some air-conditioned express services in operation. Central Bus Stand, Olcott Mawatha, Colombo 11, information, tel: (01) 328081.

GETTING AROUND

Car hire: Self-drive cars are available through **Avis**, tel: (01) 448065, but given local roads and driving conditions, a car

with driver is preferable. These are also available through Avis and most local tour agencies.

Trains: Local trains run from Colombo Fort Station to the southern suburbs, including Dehiwala and Mount Lavinia, and to the airport. Railway information, tel: (01) 435838.

Buses: Buses are cheap and frequent, but can be crowded and uncomfortable, especially during early morning and early evening rush hour. Services to all suburban points leave from stops outside Fort Railway Station. Central Bus Stand information, tel: (01) 329604/5. Air-conditioned Airport Express buses operate between the city centre and the airport, tel: (01) 687037.

Taxis: Taxis are a bargain and by far the best way of getting around unless you are on a really tight budget. Air-conditioned, metered cabs are available from Metro Radio Cabs, tel: (01) 812812, and GNTC, tel: (01) 688688.

Three-wheelers: A hybrid of motor scooter and rickshaw, these miniature taxis go every-where but are unmetered and charge tourists double the local fare as a matter of course. They are still very cheap if you agree a price before you get in.

WHERE TO STAY

Central Colombo is well-supplied with luxury hotels, most of them operated by well-known international chains. It also has plenty of

mid-range and budget places. Outside the centre, the Mount Lavinia Hotel offers a touch of class.

Central Colombo
LUXURY
Hotel Lanka Oberoi, 77 Steuart Place, Colombo 3, tel: (01) 421171, fax: (01) 449 280. Luxurious modern hotel, fine restaurant, part of the Indian-owned Oberoi group. Colombo's finest hotel.
Ceylon Inter-Continental Hotel, 48 Janadhipathi Mawatha, Colombo 1, tel: (01) 326880, fax: (01) 447326. Comfortable if rather sterile international chain hotel with very central location, high-rise with large pool.
Taj Samudra Hotel, 25 Galle Face Centra Road, Colombo 3, tel: (01) 446622, fax: (01) 446348. Fine sea views from the upper floors of this five-star hotel in the Galle Face district.
Hilton International, Lotus Road, Echelon Square, Colombo 1, tel: (01) 544544, fax: (01) 449875. Prestigious international chain hotel.

MID-RANGE
Hotel Renuka, 328 Galle Road, Colombo 3, tel: (01) 573598, fax: (01) 574137. Excellent value, medium-sized hotel with air-conditioned rooms, pool and restaurant.

BUDGET
Sea View Hotel, 15 Sea View Avenue, Colombo 3, tel/fax:

Colombo at a Glance

(01) 573570. Reliable, reasonably priced and central, but no view of the sea!

Negombo
MID-RANGE
Brown's Beach Hotel, 175 Lewis Place, Negombo, tel: (031) 20312, fax: (074) 870572. Quality resort hotel which offers excellent value for money with an attractive pool and a good buffet restaurant.

Mount Lavinia
LUXURY
Mount Lavinia Hotel, 100 Hotel Road, Mount Lavinia, tel/fax: (01) 715221. Historic hotel with 275 rooms, all with sea views, extensive beach frontage, five restaurants.

WHERE TO EAT

LUXURY
Colombo's luxury hotels all offer a choice of fine European, Japanese, Chinese and Indian/Sri Lankan restaurants.

MID-RANGE
Colombo offers countless affordable restaurants serving Chinese and Sri Lankan food. There are also several Italian and Japanese restaurants. **Cricket Club Café**, 34 Queens Road, Colombo 3, tel: (01) 501384. Snacks, meals and drinks from 09:00 until 11:00. **Sea Fish Restaurant**, 15 Sir Chittampalam Gardiner Mawatha, Colombo 2, tel: (01) 326915. Western and Sri Lankan (mainly seafood) dishes.

BUDGET
For really cheap eats, try the food stalls that appear at weekends on Galle Face. For the less daring, the **New Woodland Vegetarian Restaurant**, 108 York Street, 1st Floor, Negris Building, Colombo 1, (no tel or fax) serves clean, healthy Sri Lankan and Indian veggie specialities.

SHOPPING

The **Sri Lanka Handicrafts Board** runs department stores and shops at York Street, Colombo 1; Liberty Plaza, Colombo 3; Bauddhaloka Mawatha, Colombo 7; Sri Lanka Handlooms Emporium, Galle Road, Colombo 4; Folk Arts Centre, Sri Jayawardenapura, Kotte, Colombo, open 09.30–17.00 weekdays, 09.30–13.00 Saturdays. Good buys include silverware, brasswork, rattan-ware, brightly coloured lacquered wooden bowls, tables, walking sticks, batik cloth, handloom textiles, lace, pottery and demon masks from the south. Genuine gemstones are on sale at the **Sri Lanka Gem and Jewellery Exchange**, 310 Galle Road, Colombo 3.

TOURS AND EXCURSIONS

Organized tours to Sri Lanka's attractions and the islands of the Maldives archipelago are available from numerous tour companies in the city and the tour desks of major hotels. **Airwing Tours**, 68 Colombo Road, Negombo, tel: (031) 38116, fax: (031) 38155 and 380/85 Bullers Road, Colombo 7, tel & fax: (01) 697384. **Hemtours**, 6th Floor, Hemas House, 75 Braybrooke Place, Colombo 2, tel: (01) 300001, fax: (01) 300004. Companies specialising in birding and ecotourism include: **A Baur & Co**, Wildlife and Birdwatching Service, PO Box 11, Colombo 1, tel: (01) 320551, fax: (01) 448493. **Adventurers Lanka**, 12A Simon Mewavitharana Road, Colombo 3, tel: (01) 576474, fax: (01) 575425.

USEFUL CONTACTS

Ceylon Tourist Board, Colombo Travel Information Centre, 80 Galle Road, Colombo 3, tel: (01) 437571, fax: (01) 437953/440001. **International Airport Travel Information Centre**, Colombo, tel: (01) 252411.

COLOMBO	J	F	M	A	M	J	J	A	S	O	N	D
AVERAGE TEMP. °C	26	27	27	28	29	27	27	27	27	27	26	26
AVERAGE TEMP. °F	79	81	81	82	83	81	81	81	81	81	79	79
HOURS OF SUN DAILY	8	9	8	7	6	5	6	6	6	7	6	8
RAINFALL mm	89	69	147	231	371	224	135	109	160	348	315	147
RAINFALL in	3.5	2.7	5.8	9.1	14.6	8.8	5.3	4.3	6.3	13.7	12.4	5.8
DAYS OF RAINFALL	7	6	8	14	19	18	12	11	13	19	16	10

3
Kandy and the Hill Country

For many, the ancient highland capital of Kandy is still the true heart of Sri Lanka, where the last **Sinhalese kings** held out against the European powers, protected by the natural defences of their steep hills and dense tropical forests. Portuguese expeditions reached Kandy in the late 16th century, only to be trapped and put to the sword. The more pragmatic Dutch reduced the Kandyan kingdom by blockading its supply routes, but Kandy was finally defeated and its last king overthrown by the British in 1815.

The journey of 115km (73 miles) inland from Colombo takes up to three hours by rail or road, and as your vehicle crosses deep river valleys, negotiates numerous hairpin bends and winds upward through increasingly steep **hill country** – where cinnamon and nutmeg plantations scent the breeze, tame elephants trudge by under heavy burdens, and flying foxes like ragged umbrellas hang from high branches – it is easy to see how Kandy maintained its independence for so long. In fact, its kings banned the building of roads to the coast, to hinder would-be European conquerors still further. 'The ways are many but very narrow, so that but one can go abreast,' wrote **Robert Knox**, the Scots venturer who was held captive in Kandy for 20 years in the late 17th century.

Surrounded by cool, lush mountain scenery, Kandy is the gateway to a very different aspect of Sri Lanka, one which those visitors who restrict their stay to the country's coastal resorts never see.

INDIAN OCEAN

Central Province

Matale
Kegalla • Kandy
Nuwara Badulla
Eliya • Monaragala
Ratnapura • Province
Province of of Uva
Sabaragamuwa

DON'T MISS

*** Tooth Temple (Dalada Maligawa): this major pilgrimage site guards sacred tooth relic of the Buddha.
*** Royal Botanical Gardens: beautiful gardens laid out for kings.
*** Pinnewala Elephant Orphanage: herd of rescued elephants meets the public.
*** Horton Plains National Park: high plains landscapes and unique flora and fauna.

Opposite: *The Peradeniya Botanical Gardens, founded by a Kandyan king.*

South of Kandy, the country rises still further, to the cool green slopes of Sri Lanka's tea country around **Nuwara Eliya**, beneath the country's highest peak, **Pidurutalagala**. Here, the hills rise to an average height of more than 900m (2952ft), with several summits which rise to more than 2000m (6562ft). With its waterfalls, caves and lush woodland sheltering unique animal, bird and butterfly species, this region is a delight for walkers and explorers with an interest in Sri Lanka's natural wonders as well as its ancient cultural heritage.

KANDY

At 500m (1640ft) above sea level, Sri Lanka's second city has a climate that comes as a pleasantly cool contrast to hot and humid Colombo. Amid lush green fields and plantations – evidence of the region's well-watered fertility – the city stands within a loop of the **Mahaweli**

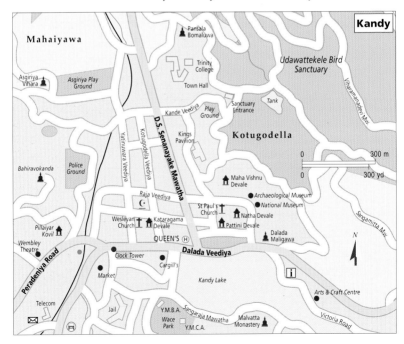

Ganga, one of Sri Lanka's more substantial rivers, on the north shore of Kandy Lake, an artificial reservoir which was completed in 1807, during the reign of the last king of Kandy, Sri Wickrama Rajasinha. He kept his concubines on the artificial island in the centre of the lake, and had a number of his enemies drowned slowly, tied to stakes and gasping for air as the waters of the lake rose.

Above: *Waterfalls, like these at Nuwara Eliya, are typical of the lush hill country.*

Tooth Temple (Dalada Maligawa) ***

Overlooking the north shore of **Kandy Lake**, in the centre of town, the Temple of the Tooth is a place of pilgrimage for millions of devout Buddhists from all over Sri Lanka, and is regarded by Buddhist Sri Lankans as the treasury of their entire culture. Sri Lanka's premiers and presidents traditionally deliver their first post-election speeches from its balcony, and lesser politicians too make thanksgiving visits to the temple on election.

The **Tooth Relic** itself is claimed to have come to Sri Lanka some 1600 years ago, when a certain princess from southern India brought it to Anuradhapura, which was then the most powerful kingdom in Sri Lanka. As kings and kingdoms rose and fell, it finally ended up in Kandy around AD1100. Over centuries, as the Sinhalese came under increasing pressure from invasion, it became more and more symbolic of Sri Lankan freedom and independence.

The existing temple was begun in 1687 and added to by a succession of Kandyan kings over the next 95 years. Painted pale rose, surrounded by walls adorned with elephant carvings and a moat, and roofed with terracotta tiles, the temple receives a steady flow of pilgrims and tourists.

CLIMATE

The rainiest months in the highlands are June to December, when rainfall at Nuwara Eliya reaches or exceeds 200mm (8in), reaching a high of 300mm (12in) in July. Maximum temperature hovers around 22°C (72°F) year-round, reaching or exceeding 30°C from January to May and one or two degrees below this level for the rest of the year. **Average temperature** is noticeably cooler than on the coast, at only **16°C** (61°F) in Kandy and as low as 16°C (61°F) in Nuwara Eliya, thanks to cool night-time temperatures.

Above: *The Temple of the Tooth at Kandy shelters one of the holiest relics of the Buddha in the entire world, and attracts pilgrims from all over Sri Lanka.*

WOMEN'S RIGHTS

Foreign visitors to Kandy in its heyday were amazed – and outraged – at the freedom enjoyed by its women, who arguably had greater control over their own affairs than their European contemporaries. The Dutch, Portuguese and British were particularly offended to see that not only might Kandyan men have several wives, so might women have **several husbands**. They also had the right to divorce their husbands, and the right to own property, centuries before their sisters in the west achieved such freedom.

Dress modestly (no shorts or singlets) and leave your shoes at the entrance before joining the never-ending line that shuffles through the decorated halls and eventually moves into the darkened, gilt-roofed relic chamber which is the temple's holy of holies. Within, two monks stand sentinel before a gold reliquary, all that you will be allowed to see of the holy molar. Don't leave, however, without seeing the **library** of *ola* (palm-leaf) manuscripts housed in the pagoda-like **moat tower**. The temple is open daily 24 hours; the library is open 09:00–17:00 daily.

National Museum **

Next to the Temple of the Tooth, the Kandy National Museum once housed the concubines of the Kings of Kandy and now contains a clutter of royal and noble relics including thrones, sceptres and ceremonial swords, dating from the 17th and 18th centuries, before the kingdom's final decline. It was here that the Kandyan chiefs finally surrendered to the British in 1815. After inviting them in to depose the unpopular king Sri Wickrama Rajasinha, the rebel chiefs attempted to dismiss the British with perfunctory thanks, only to find that their new rulers had no intention of leaving. Open Saturday–Thursday 09:00–17:00.

Trinity College Chapel *

Trinity College, standing in manicured grounds off D S Senanayake Mawatha, was founded in 1872 to provide education on English lines for the children of British planters and administrators and for Sri Lankan converts to the Anglican church. It is still the country's foremost Christian educational establishment. The chapel, with its granite columns carved with traditional Sinhalese patterns as well as the crests of Oxford and Cambridge colleges, is a remarkable blend of western and Sinhalese architectural influences, with wooden doorways and roof beams carved by local craftsmen, a pantiled roof, and overhanging eaves that echo the design of the Tooth Temple. The work of the college's vice principal, it was begun in 1922 to mark the 50th anniversary of the foundation of Trinity College. The huge murals within, depicting stories from the Bible, are the work of the aptly named **David Paynter**, one of Sri Lanka's most famous artists.

> **ROBERT KNOX**
>
> The son of a Scottish merchant adventurer, the master of the frigate *Anne*, Robert Knox was taken prisoner with his father when their ship landed for repairs at Trincomalee, and was held captive by the King of Kandy, Rajasinha II, from 1660–80. His account of that time, *An Historical Relation of Ceylon*, was published in 1681 and is still one of the authoritative sources on the kingdom of Kandy before its conquest by Britain.

Below: *A sign of commitment at the Udawattekele Bird Sanctuary.*

Udawattekele Bird Sanctuary **

About 1km (0.6 miles) east of Trinity College, off Wewelpitiya Road, this is one of Sri Lanka's more accessible bird sanctuaries. It is a stretch of wilderness only a stone's throw from the city centre with towering forest giants and creepers giving shelter to bird species including Layard's parakeet, Sri Lanka hanging parrot, yellow-fronted barbet, black-capped bulbul, emerald dove, three species of kingfisher, chestnut-headed bee eater and Tickells's blue flycatcher. It is also the home of scores of macaque monkeys, and huge, vividly painted butterflies float across the paths. Open daily 08:00–17:30.

O, GREAT KING THE BIRDS OF THE AIR AND BEASTS HAVE AN EQUAL RIGHT TO LIVE AND MOVE ABOUT IN ANY PART OF THIS LAND AS THOU. THE LAND BELONGS TO THE PEOPLE AND ALL OTHER BEINGS AND THOU ARE ONLY THE GUARDIAN OF IT. — ARAHAT MAHINDA.

DONATED BY THE LIONS CLUB OF KANDY.

Royal Botanical Gardens ***

About 6km (4 miles) southwest of the town centre at Peradeniya on the Colombo highway, close to the banks of the Mahaweli Ganga, these gorgeous gardens were first planted and laid out for King Kirthi Sri Rajasingha (1747–1780) and cover some 60ha (150 acres) of trees, lawns and flowering shrubs, including a 20-ha (50-acre) **arboretum** of more than 10,000 trees. Under British rule, the royal park became a botanical garden in 1821 and is the largest of Sri Lanka's three main botanical gardens. Here, exotic crops such as coffee, tea, nutmeg, rubber and cinchona (quinine) – all of which later became important to Sri Lanka's economy – were tested. Sights include a **palm avenue** planted by the British in 1905. Another British import was the enormous spreading **Java fig** which sprawls across the lawn, grown from a sapling brought from the East Indies.

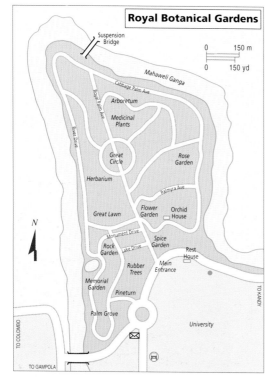

Royal Botanical Gardens

Suspension Bridge

0   150 m
0   150 yd

Mahaweli Ganga

Cabbage Palm Ave

Royal Palm Ave

Arboretum

River Drive

Medicinal Plants

Great Circle

Rose Garden

Herbarium

Palmyra Ave

Great Lawn

Flower Garden

Orchid House

Monument Drive

Spice Garden

Rock Garden

Lake Drive

Rest House

Rubber Trees

Main Entrance

Memorial Garden

Pineturn

Palm Grove

University

N

TO COLOMBO

TO GAMPOLA

TO KANDY

The gardens also have stands of towering **bamboos** from Burma, Japan, China and the East Indies, and a fine collection of **orchids** from Sri Lanka and further afield.

In the centre of the gardens is an **artificial lake** in the shape of the island of Sri Lanka, beside which a white-domed rotunda commemorates George Gardner, superintendent of the gardens in the mid-19th century.

The Royal Botanical Gardens are worth a visit, and are open daily from 07:30 until 17:00.

AROUND KANDY

The lush countryside around Kandy is dotted with small Buddhist and Hindu shrines and temples, while just off the Colombo highway, the Pinnewala Elephant Orphanage is well worth stopping at on the way to or from the coast. A small donation (usually anything from 20 to 100 rupees) is required to visit the temples.

Embekke Devale *

About 6km (4 miles) southwest of Peradeniya and 3 km (2 miles) east of the main road to Nuwara Eliya, around 13km (8 miles) from the centre of Kandy, this small Buddhist temple dates from the 14th century and is graced by **wooden columns** elaborately sculpted with birds, dancers, acrobats and wrestlers. Open during daylight hours.

Lankatilake Temple *

Just under 2km (1.5 miles) on foot north of the Embekke Temple (the last stretch is an energetic ascent of steps cut into the crag on which the temple stands), the Lankatilake Temple is predominantly a Hindu place of worship but also has Buddhist **frescoes**, a **Buddha** image, and stone **elephant** carvings. Open during daylight hours only.

Gadaldeniye Temple *

Approximately 3km (2 miles) on foot or by bus north of Lankatilake, and 1km (0.6 miles) south of the main Colombo road, this is a mainly Buddhist temple with a Hindu shrine attached. It contains some interesting **Buddha images** and **frescoes** from the 14th century. Open during daylight hours.

Above: *The Gadaldeniye Temple near Kandy is sacred to both Buddhist and Hindu worshippers.*

> **ESALA FESTIVAL**
>
> The **full moon day** of Esala (July/August) is the high point of ten nights of drumming, dancing and processions, with Kandyan dancers and drummers in traditional costume, chiefs in medieval court dress, and more than a hundred elephants in colourful trappings parading through the streets of Kandy, Sri Lanka's hill capital, in a vivid re-enactment of life in the central highlands before the British conquest.

Right: *Elephants at the Pinnewala Elephant Orphanage enjoy a daily bath with their trainers in the muddy waters of the nearby river.*
Opposite: *The red-wattled lapwing, one of the many rare and endemic bird species found in Sri Lanka's wetlands and fields.*

ELEPHANTS

Domesticated elephants have served Sri Lankans in peace and war for more than 2000 years. They are **symbols of power** and **wealth**, and stories of the deeds of royal war elephants in battle abound in the ancient annals of the kings of Kandy and Anuradhapura. Gorgeously caparisoned elephants are the most spectacular aspect of religious processions like the *Esala Perahera* in Kandy. Sri Lanka's elephants are sadly diminished, not least because of the bloodthirsty stupidity of British hunters and planters in colonial times. Today there are around 2500 elephants in the wild, with some 500 in captivity. Habitat loss, and the continuing guerrilla war in Sri Lanka's deep jungles, pose **continuing threats**, though commendable conservation projects are in place, including the creation of 'corridor' reserves to allow elephants to migrate between larger national parks.

Pinnewala Elephant Orphanage ★★★

A visit to the elephant orphanage near Kegalla, 20km (12 miles) west of Kandy on the Colombo highway, where young **orphaned or abandoned elephants** are cared for, is a must. The herd usually numbers about 50, from tiny infants (tiny in elephant terms, that is) to hefty adolescents and young adults. Most have lost their parents either to poachers or road accidents, but some have simply become separated from their parental herd. The best time to visit is between 10:00 and midday, and 14:00 and 16:00, when the keepers bring their charges down to the river to bathe and play. Habituated to humans and domestic elephants, most of the orphans join the ranks of Sri Lanka's many working elephants when they reach maturity, as they cannot easily be returned to the wild. Open daily, dawn to dusk.

On the road from the highway to the orphanage, look out for the scores of **flying foxes** (fruit bats) hanging high in the treetops beside the river or, at sunset, spreading their wings.

NUWARA ELIYA

Nuwara Eliya, 100km (62 miles) south of Kandy and among some of Sri Lanka's most verdant hillsides at 1800m (5906ft) above sea level, is more reminiscent of the days of the **English tea planters** than any other place in Sri Lanka. This is hardly surprising, for Nuwara Eliya

was built entirely during the 19th century and its architecture mimics that of an English country town, with red-brick walls and mock-Tudor half-timbering. Though the British planters and officials who found Nuwara Eliya a congenial place to escape from the heat of the lowlands are long gone, Sri Lanka's well-to-do still migrate to its **cool climes** during the hottest parts of the year and especially during the Sinhalese New Year holidays in April. With mountain forests, wilderness areas and national parks in easy reach – starting only 8km (5 miles) from the centre – Nuwara Eliya is a very popular base for birdwatchers and ecotourists. It also has an adequate 18-hole golf course.

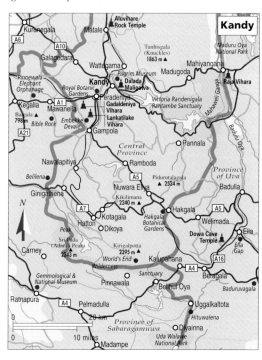

Right: *White-bearded langurs are among several monkey species found in Sri Lanka's forests.*
Opposite: *View over the Horton Plains, a high misty plateau quite unlike the rest of the highlands.*

THE *RAMAYANA*

The **Hindu epic**, the *Ramayana*, recounts the tale of how Sita, wife of the god Rama, was kidnapped and carried off the Lanka by the ten-headed demon king Ravana. Local legend says the Sita Eliya Temple, 1km north of Hakgala, is where she was held captive, and that the dips in the rock opposite are the footprints of the demon king's mount. Eventually, Rama, at the head of an army of monkeys led by his ally, the monkey-king Hanuman, defeated and killed Ravana and rescued his queen, a victory celebrated at the Hindu festival of *Diwali*.

Victoria Park *

The ornamental park in the centre of town, separated from the golf course by New Bazaar Street, is a good place to spot a number of hill country **bird species**. Look out for yellow-eared bulbul, pied thrush, Kashmir flycatcher, Indian blue robin, grey tit, Indian pitta, Pacific swallow and, along the stream that runs through the park, green sandpiper. Open from dawn till dusk.

Pidurutalagala *

Sri Lanka's highest peak, also known as Mount Pedro, rises 2524m (8281ft) above sea level, immediately behind the town. Unfortunately, the path to the summit, which is the site of Sri Lanka's main television transmitter, is closed to visitors for security reasons. For a view of the summit, and a superb panorama of the surrounding hills and plantations, you can walk to the top of the picturesquely named **Single Tree Mountain**, south of town off the Badulla road, in about 90 minutes.

Hakgala Botanical Gardens **

After the Royal Botanical Gardens at Peradeniya, Hakgala, 10km (6 miles) south of Nuwara Eliya, is the second most important garden in Sri Lanka. Though on a smaller scale than those at Peradeniya, Hakgala's plantations of roses, shrubs, ferns and montane woodland are delightfully located, with scenic views. Open daily from 07:30 to 17:00.

Above the gardens, a forest trail leads into **virgin woodland** – the home of a troop of purple-faced leaf monkeys, a species endemic to Sri Lanka, and to endemic bird species including the Sri Lanka white-eye, Sri Lanka wood pigeon, and Sri Lanka whistling thrush.

Horton Plains National Park ***

The landscapes of this high, misty plateau, some 20km (12 miles) south of Nuwara Eliya and up to 2400m (7874ft) above sea level, are unique in Sri Lanka, combining mountain grassland with areas of miniature 'elfin' forest – dwarf forms of trees and shrubs adapted to the cool climate and skimpy soil of the plains. Above the plateau rise the summits of **Kirigalpotta** and **Totapola**, at 2395m (7858ft) and 2357m (7733ft) respectively, they are Sri Lanka's second- and third-highest peaks.

Wildlife includes sambar, which keep to the edge of wooded areas, bear monkey, often seen and heard in forested areas, and giant squirrel and leopard, which are shy and very rarely seen. Many visitors make a beeline for **World's End**, the 700m (2300ft) drop-off that forms an abrupt southern boundary to the plains. For the best views, arrive at sunrise, before the mist that often shrouds the slopes below has had time to form.

> **RUBBER**
>
> Rubber, still an important crop which accounts for **3 per cent of Sri Lanka's exports**, came to the island from its native South America by way of Kew Gardens near London, where British botanists raised thousands of seedlings from seeds smuggled out of Brazil to break the Brazilian monopoly on rubber. The first rubber trees were planted in the 1890s and by 1901 some 1012ha (2500 acres) of land in the foothills of the central highlands were planted in rubber. Today, more than 242,816ha (600,000 acres) is devoted to the growing of rubber.

SRI PADA

Thousands of devout be-
lievers – mainly Buddhists,
but also Hindus, Muslims and
Christians – climb Sri Pada
(**Adam's Peak**) during the
pilgrimage season each year.
Observances start on the full-
moon day of December and
continue until the full-moon
day of April the following
year. **Sunrise**, seen from the
peak, is one of the great
sights of Sri Lanka, but
making the climb during
pilgrimage season takes
many hours longer than
doing it in other months.

Below: *During the
pilgrimage season, the
summit of Adam's Peak
draws thousands of
pilgrims from all of
Sri Lanka's religions.*

Adam's Peak (Sri Pada) & Peak Wilderness Sanctuary ***

Horton Plains National Park borders the Peak
Wilderness Sanctuary, a crescent, 40km (25-mile) swathe
of montane forest that can be approached from
Dalhousie, 25km (15 miles) west of Nuwara Eliya, off the
main Nuwara Eliya–Colombo road, or from Carney, 8km
(5 miles) north of Ratnapura.

Adam's Peak, in the centre of the sanctuary, is recognized as a sacred place by all Sri Lanka's religions.
Muslims and some Christians say the 'footprint' in the
rock atop the rust-red, 2243m (7359ft) peak is where
Adam first set foot on earth after being exiled from Eden.
Other Christians say it is the footprint of St Thomas, who
brought Christianity to southern India in the 1st century
AD, while to Hindus it is the mark of Lord Shiva.
Buddhists, however, who have covered the original
'print' with a larger than life concrete copy, say it was
made by the Buddha on his third visit to Sri Lanka. In
the pilgrimage season, from December until April, thousands trek to the top each day, taking all day to complete
the 8km (5-mile) ascent from Dalhousie village. At other
times, the ascent will take you around four hours.

Left: *Precious and semiprecious stones such as diamonds, rubies, sapphires and emeralds can be bought and tested at the Gem and Jewellery Exchange in Colombo.*

RATNAPURA

Roughly 100km (64 miles) southeast of Colombo on the outskirts of the hill country, Ratnapura is known as Sri Lanka's gemstone capital. The town has fine views of Adam's Peak on the eastern horizon, and is surrounded by thickly forested hills. Precious stones are dug by hand from small pockets of gem-bearing gravel in the hills and fields around Ratnapura, and include sapphires, rubies, moonstones, and a variety of semiprecious stones such as beryl, zircon, garnet and quartz, all of which you will be offered on the street by shady looking characters offering a 'special price'. As many naive buyers have found, there are no bargains. Precious and semi-precious stones are also sold loose by a number of more reputable stores, but prices are little different from those in Colombo or indeed the rest of the world.

Gemmological and National Museum *

At Getangama on the outskirts of town, this privately run museum and showroom offers a wide range of stones for sale, and you can also watch the raw stones being cut and polished. Open 09:00–17:30 daily.

BUYING GEMS

The best and safest way to buy Sri Lankan gemstones is at the government-run Gem and Jewellery Exchange in Colombo, which is operated by the National Gem and Jewellery Authority to assist the export of precious stones. The Exchange also has a gem-testing laboratory and assay centre, so you can find out if any stones you have bought are the real thing; 310 Galle Road, Colombo 1, tel: (01) 326203.

Kandy and the Hill Country at a Glance

The hill country is most pleasant from September to late April. From May to September, heavy rains make travel slower and less easy and visiting the mainly open-air attractions of the region less appealing.

By rail: Trains run between Colombo Fort Railway Station and Kandy up to nine times daily. Trains also connect Kandy with Nanu Oya (for Nuwara Eliya) and Ohiya (for Horton Plains), on a loop that ends at Badulla, on the eastern fringe of the hill country. Train information and reservations: Fort Railway Station, information, tel: (01) 435838.

By road: Buses connect Colombo with Kandy via the main A1 highway, and link Kandy with Nuwara Eliya, Hakgala and Ohiya (for Horton Plains) via the A5.
A separate bus route runs southeast on the A8 to connect Colombo and Ratnapura. There are also buses between Ratnapura and Matara, on the south coast. Heading north, express buses connect Kandy with Anuradhapura.

Given the small size of all the hill country towns, including Kandy, the best way of exploring each town is on foot. Other options include three-wheelers and taxis. As usual, agree the fare before setting off. Local buses offer a cheaper way of getting to outlying temples and other sights.

The few luxury hotels in the hill country are in Kandy and Nuwara Eliya, but there are comfortable mid-range hotels and affordable budget guesthouses throughout the region.

Kandy
LUXURY

Mahaweli Beach Hotel, 35 PBA Weerakoon Mawatha, PO Box 78, Kandy, tel: (074) 472727, fax: (074) 232068. The most luxurious place to stay in the region, with huge outdoor pool, tennis courts, billiard room, and in-room facilities.

Queen's Hotel, 3 Sangamitta Mawatha, Kandy, tel: (08) 23329, fax: (08) 223079. Reminiscent of the elegance of the colonial era, used by Earl Mountbatten as his hot weather hill country headquarters during World War II.

MID-RANGE

Chalet Hotel, 32 Gregory's Road, Kandy, tel: (08) 2234571, no fax. Comfortable hotel near the town centre.

BUDGET

Hotel Suisse, 30 Sangaraja Mawatha, Kandy, tel/fax: (08) 32083. Good value for money, professionally managed, reasonable facilities and very clean.

Nuwara Eliya
LUXURY

St Andrew's Hotel, 10 St Andrew's Drive, Nuwara Eliya, tel: (052) 22445, fax: (052) 23153. Comfortable, recently modernized accommodation in a colonial-style hotel – originally the 19th-century clubhouse of the region's Scottish planters, and built in the style of the Royal Golf Club at St Andrew's, Scotland. Four-poster beds, attractive garden.

Grand Hotel, Grand Hotel Road, Nuwara Eliya, tel: (052) 2884, fax: (052) 2265. Nuwara Eliya's poshest hotel, next to the golf course. Billiard room, bars; reeks of the jolly old British Empire.

MID-RANGE

The Tea Factory, Kandapola, Nuwara Eliya, tel: (052) 3600, fax: (070) 522105. Hotel of character located in the restored buildings of a former tea plantation. Good value.

BUDGET

Galway Forest Lodge, 89 Havelock Drive, Nuwara Eliya, tel: (052) 3739, fax: (052) 2978. Good value for money, friendly management, a touch of class for the price.

Horton Plains
MID-RANGE

Farr Inn, Horton Plains National Park, tel: (072) 52575, for reservations contact Ceylon Hotels Corporation, 411 Galle Road, Colombo 4, tel: (01)

Kandy and the Hill Country at a Glance

503497, fax: (01) 503504. A former colonial rest-house in the centre of the plains, now a cosy guesthouse with comfortable rooms, good restaurant.

Ratnapura
BUDGET
Ratnaloka Tour Inn, Kosgala, Kahangama, Ratnapura, tel: (045) 2455. Adequate, reasonable value for money; the only place to stay in Ratnapura!

WHERE TO EAT

Sadly, the region boasts no luxury restaurants, though there are plenty of good-value, mid-range places to eat, and innumerable budget restaurants. In the mid range, virtually all serve Chinese as well as Sri Lankan dishes.

Kandy
MID-RANGE
Mahaweli Beach Hotel, (see *Where to Stay*) has an excellent and not exorbitant Sri Lankan restaurant, and a poolside international buffet.
Flower Song Restaurant, 137 Kotugodella Veediya, Kandy, tel: (08) 23628, no fax. Chinese dishes and Sri Lankan specialities, air conditioning, and – unusually – a wine list.
Rodney Peppers, 136 DS Senanayake Vidiya, Kandy, tel: (08) 25616, no fax. Chinese and Sri Lankan dishes.

BUDGET
Lyon Café, 27 Peradeniye Road, tel: (08) 23073. Very cheap, clean and efficient, popular with budget travellers. Chinese and Sri Lankan rice dishes, noodles and curries.

Nuwara Eliya
MID-RANGE
Grand Hotel (see *Where to Stay*) has excellent breakfast, lunch and dinner buffets most days, with a choice of Sri Lankan and international dishes.

Ratnapura
BUDGET
Nilani Tourist Restaurant, 202 Pothgul Vihara Mawatha, Ratnapura, tel: (045) 2116. Best of a bunch of humdrum eating places serving the usual Sri Lankan and Chinese staples.

TOURS AND EXCURSIONS

Kandy is the gateway to the hill country for travellers from Colombo, and a number of tour companies offer group and individual tailor-made tours around the region's main sights. Tour companies in Colombo (see *Colombo At A Glance*, p 44–45) also offer a range of itineraries combining the high points of the hill country with the ruined cities and temples of the Cultural Triangle, to the north, and the beaches of the south or west coasts. **JF Tours & Travels**, 189 New Buller's Road, Colombo 4, tel: (01) 589402, fax: (01) 580507, organizes steam train journeys between Colombo and Kandy aboard the *Viceroy Special*, as well as tours by rail throughout the country. In Kandy, you can contact: **Travel Network**, 8 Cross Street, tel: (08) 224932, fax: (08) 224628.

SHOPPING

Kandy has excellent shopping opportunities. In Nuwara Eliya, there's a smaller range of shops along New Bazaar Street. In Ratnapura (reputed to be the country's gem capital) unmounted gemstones sold in a number of 'gem museums' are not necessarily any cheaper than mounted stones sold in Colombo and Kandy. Gems offered by touts at 'bargain' prices can turn out to be poor-quality stones.

USEFUL CONTACTS
Ceylon Tourist Board, Travel Information Centre, Headman's Lodge, 3 Dewa Veediya, Kandy, tel: (08) 222661.

KANDY	J	F	M	A	M	J	J	A	S	O	N	D
AVERAGE TEMP. °C	14	14	15	16	17	16	16	16	16	16	16	15
AVERAGE TEMP. °F	57	57	58	60	62	60	60	60	60	60	60	58
HOURS OF SUN DAILY	8	9	8	7	6	5	6	6	6	7	6	8
RAINFALL mm	170	43	109	119	175	277	300	196	226	269	241	203
RAINFALL in	6.7	1.7	4.3	4.7	6.9	10.9	11.8	7.7	8.9	10.6	9.5	8
DAYS OF RAINFALL	13	6	11	15	18	25	25	22	20	22	22	17

4
Galle and the Southwest

The coast south of Colombo is Sri Lanka's most popular holiday resort area, with fine beaches of golden sand lined with coconut palms, where traditional outrigger canoes are still hauled up in front of gleaming new holiday hotels favoured by visitors from northern Europe and Asia. Yet, attractive as these resorts are, Sri Lanka has experienced nothing like the tourism explosion that has rocked so many tropical dream destinations, and there are still miles of uncrowded coastline to explore, while within a few kilometres of the resorts tourism has had little impact. The beaches are the biggest attraction of this part of the island, but the region has more to offer than lounging beneath the palms. Inshore, there are easily accessible coral gardens. Offshore, there are some excellent dive sites, both on reefs and around wrecks. Inland, the **Sinharaja Biosphere Reserve** takes visitors deeper into the unchanged virgin forest.

Galle, the largest town in the region, is full of history, and Sri Lanka's small size means that a stay in one of the beach resorts of the southwest can easily be combined with sightseeing in the hill country or the ancient cities of the Cultural Triangle. The biggest concentration of resort hotels is in the area closest to Colombo and its international airport, between Beruwala and Bentota, where several fishing villages have merged into a string of attractive low-rise resorts surrounded by boutiques, beach bars and restaurants. Resort hotels also cluster around **Hikkaduwa**, a little further south, and at **Koggala**, east of Galle.

INDIAN OCEAN

Southern Province

Galle

DON'T MISS

*** **Bentota:** Sri Lanka's top hotels, between a fine beach and a lovely river.
*** **Hikkaduwa:** the country's biggest and liveliest holiday resort beaches, with good coral and diving.
*** **Galle:** old Dutch town within massive ramparts.
** **Sinharaja Biosphere Reserve:** a slice of virgin forest sheltering many endemic bird species.

Opposite: *The famous stilt fishermen of Sri Lanka's south coast.*

Above: *The long stretch of Bentota beach is one of the finest on the island.*

BERUWALA

Just 60km (38 miles) south of Colombo on the main west coast road, Beruwala is the gateway to the southwest's string of holiday resorts, and many package holiday-makers travel no further than this, perfectly content with its combination of mid-range hotel accommodation, fine sandy beaches and plenty of bars and restaurants serving international dishes, fine seafood and Sri Lankan dishes. Tourism, however, has not entirely taken over. Fragile-looking outrigger canoes with triangular sails and palm-thatched deckhouses are still drawn up on the beach either side of the Bentota River, which officially separates Beruwala from the adjoining resort strip of Bentota. Just north of the hotel colony, the **Kechimalai Mosque** is built on the spot where the first Muslim traders from the Middle East landed and settled in AD1024. Just south of Beruwela, at Alutgama on the north bank of the Bentota River, there is a colourful and odorous early morning fish market, where outrigger canoes unload their glistening catch.

ORUVAS

The **outrigger canoes** called *oruvas* have been used by fishermen off Sri Lanka's shores for more than 2000 years and although they are gradually being replaced by more modern vessels there are still plenty of them around. You'll see them drawn up on beaches everywhere, or beating out to the fishing grounds under sail. Built from local hardwoods and regularly given a protective coating of coconut- or shark-liver oil, they can have a working life of up to 30 years.

BENTOTA

Like neighbouring Beruwela, Bentota is dominated by package tourism but the hotels are somewhat newer and more sophisticated. The best stand in splendid isolation on the narrow peninsula between the Bentota River and the sea, with palm-fringed beaches on both the seaward and river sides.

Kosgoda Turtle Hatchery *

About 5km (3 miles) south of Bentota, at the fishing hamlet of Kosgoda, the hatchery releases thousands of hatchling green and leatherback turtles into the wild after incubating them in fenced-off areas safe from predators. Open daily 09:00–17:00.

AMBALANGODA

Ambalangoda, 24km (15 miles) south of Beruwela, is a quiet town which has as yet escaped the attentions of the tourism development industry, though it has a beach to equal those to the north. The main attraction here, however, is the thriving mask and puppet-making industry, making colourful and grotesque *raksha*, *kolam* and *sanni* masks for Sri Lanka's many festivals, processions, and dance-dramas.

Mask Museum **

This private museum and shop is on Ambalangoda's main street 800m (875yd) north of the village centre and is run by one of the village's noted mask-makers. On display are masks symbolizing all the characters (demons, gods, heroes and villains) who appear in masked dances and processions. Open daily 09:00–17:00.

TURTLES

Bentota's turtle hatcheries are popular tourist attractions where visitors croon over tiny hatchling turtles and pay a small fee to release one into the open sea. The eggs are collected by fishermen and hatched in areas protected from hungry pigs and dogs, but some conservationists now argue this type of hatchery does as much harm as good. Bay turtles normally hatch at night and on reaching the sea swim frantically into deeper, safer waters. If kept in tanks after hatching, then released in daylight, their survival chances may be reduced. The hatcheries are no substitute for protecting the nesting areas used by the turtles for millennia.

Below: *Beruwala is one of the closest beach resorts to the capital.*

HIKKADUWA

About 10km (6 miles) to the south of Ambalangoda,
Hikkaduwa is the newest and liveliest of the southwest
coast beach resorts. Unlike Beruwala and Bentota, it is
not completely dominated by large resort hotels, and
although it now spreads for some 5km (3 miles) along
the coast, its accommodation mix includes small family-
run guesthouses as well as larger hotels. There's
excellent **snorkelling** just offshore and a number of dive
sites for more serious scuba divers further out to sea,
while good surf to the south of town attracts surfers.

Coral Gardens ***

Even if you're not a scuba diver, Hikkaduwa offers
underwater delights. Only 200m (219yd) offshore, in
shallow water no more than 4m (13ft) deep, a reef protects an expanse of
brilliant coral populat-
ed by vividly colourful
reef fish and even the
occasional turtle. It is
perfect snorkelling ter-
ritory, but for the less
confident, glass bot-
tomed boats also
operate from the beach.

Telwatta Bird
Sanctuary *

Just inland from the
main coastal highway,
2km (1.5 miles) south
of Hikkaduwa, this
small lakeside bird
sanctuary offers acces-
sible bird viewing and
is especially rich in
waterfowl and shore-
birds such as the green
sandpiper.

GALLE

Galle, 116km (74 miles) south of Colombo, on the southwest corner of the island, is the largest town in the region. Until the British conquest it was the **most important port** on the island of Sri Lanka, appearing in European histories as early as AD545. By the time of the great Arab traveller and writer Ibn Batuta, who landed here in the 13th century, it was firmly established as an entrepôt for commerce between Sri Lanka and the Arab world.

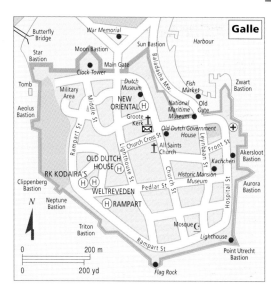

Conquered by the Portuguese in 1505, then by the Dutch in 1640, the town was extensively fortified and the lines of its fortifications – added to by the British through to World War II – can be clearly seen. These centuries-old ramparts and bastions are being excavated and conserved, and a 3km (2-mile) stretch has already been restored.

One of the best preserved colonial-era cities in Southeast Asia, Galle has been declared a **World Heritage City** and the Sri Lankan government's depart-ment of archaeology has taken on the herculean task of restoring as much as possible of the old part of the city to pristine condition.

Standing on a peninsula with a naturally sheltered anchorage on its east side, Galle has both a fine harbour and excellent natural defences. Inside its ring of ram-parts are numerous buildings dating from the Dutch era, including the Old Dutch Government House (now the offices of a shipping company), the Governor's House (now a hotel), and the Groote Kerk (Great Church), still in use by worshippers.

Opposite: *Coconut palms provide shade on all of Sri Lanka's beaches.*

TRADE ROUTES

The Portuguese and Dutch merchantmen who arrived off Sri Lanka's shores in the 16th and 17th centuries were by no means the first western navigators to arrive. The island was known to the Greeks as Taprobane, and appeared on the charts of the mysterious east drawn by the cartographer Ptolemy of Alexandria in the 3rd century BC. Muslim traders from the Gulf called it Serendib, and had established trading depots around the coast cen-turies before the Portuguese came on the scene.

Above: *This aerial view of Galle's Dutch Fort shows its massive ramparts.*

The Dutch Fort ***

A continuous rampart, built by the Dutch from the mid-17th century onward and added to by the British, encircles the city, interrupted by 14 massive bastions. The best way to see the fort is to walk the length of the walls (90 minutes), and the best time to do it is around sunset. Start at the most impressive section, where the Star, Moon and Sun bastions glower forbiddingly over the neck of the peninsula. The ramparts south of the harbour are pierced by the Old Gate, above which is a British coat of arms (on the inner side, the gate is crowned by the initials of the Dutch East India Company, VOC, and its coat of arms), and south of the harbour the Zwart (Black) Bastion is believed to be the only surviving part of the original Portuguese fortifications. The circuit of the walls continues via the Akersloot and Aurora bastions to the Point Utrecht bastion, topped by a modern lighthouse, then to Flag Rock, the southernmost point of the walls, before looping back north through the Triton, Neptune, Clippenberg and Aeolus bastions. The final section between the Aeolus and Star bastions is closed, as it is part of a military base. While some of the bastions retain their original Dutch names, the Triton, Aeolus, Neptune and Aurora bastions were renamed by the British in honour of the Royal Navy ships of the line which took part in the British seizure of Sri Lanka from the Dutch during the Napoleonic Wars.

Dutch Museum *

For a peep into life in the days of the Dutch East India Company, look into this small museum at 31 Leynbaan Street. Housed in a restored Dutch mansion of the time, it contains paintings, prints, documents, furniture and ceramics from the Dutch colonial era. Open Saturday–Thursday 09:00–17:00.

EARLY TOURISTS

Modern holiday-makers follow in the footsteps of some of the great wanderers of antiquity. The Chinese traveller **Fa-Hsien** visited Anuradhapura in AD412 and wrote an account of the island's wealth – he called it the 'Island of Jewels'. **Marco Polo**, who knew it as 'Serendib', visited it on his way home from China to Venice in 1292, and the Arabic cartographer **Ibn Batuta** visited the Muslim settlement at Galle in 1344. In the 19th century the American author **Mark Twain** was impressed by the island's 'tropical splendours of bloom, of blossom, and Oriental conflagrations of costume!'

New Oriental Hotel **

Built in 1684 as the official headquarters of the Dutch Governor, this elegant building became an inn for Dutch merchants and officers in the early 18th century, making it Sri Lanka's oldest hotel. The ghosts of former residents seem to linger around the elegantly faded old bar and billiard room. Somerset Maugham would have felt at home here, and it's the ideal place for a refreshing drink after walking round the ramparts.

Above: *The prickly jackfruit is said to be the largest fruit in the world.*
Below: *The Groote Kerk in Galle is a Dutch relic.*

Groote Kerk (Great Church) **

The original 'Great Church', the main church of the Dutch community, was built in 1640. The existing building replaced it in 1755, and its floor contains tombstones from the original cemetery. Open during usual church hours.

National Maritime Museum *

There is a small museum housed in the Old Gatehouse, with a small collection of shabby ship models, charts and other maritime memorabilia. Usually open from 09:00 to 17:00.

UNAWATUNA

Unawatuna, less than 5km (3 miles) southward around
the coast from Galle, is a beach resort waiting to happen.
If not for the troubles of the 1980s and 1990s, this 4km
(2.5-mile) sweep of palm-fringed sand – said by some to
be among the twelve best beaches in the world – would
no doubt already have gone the way of Beruwala,
Bentota and Hikkaduwa. As it is, Unawatuna, while no
longer the well-kept secret of a handful of die-hard back-
packers and divers, is still far from over-developed.
Attractions include sheltered waters for swimming, and
an accessible, reasonably well-preserved coral reef for
snorkelling. For scuba divers, there are several wreck
dives only 20–30 minutes away from the beach by boat.

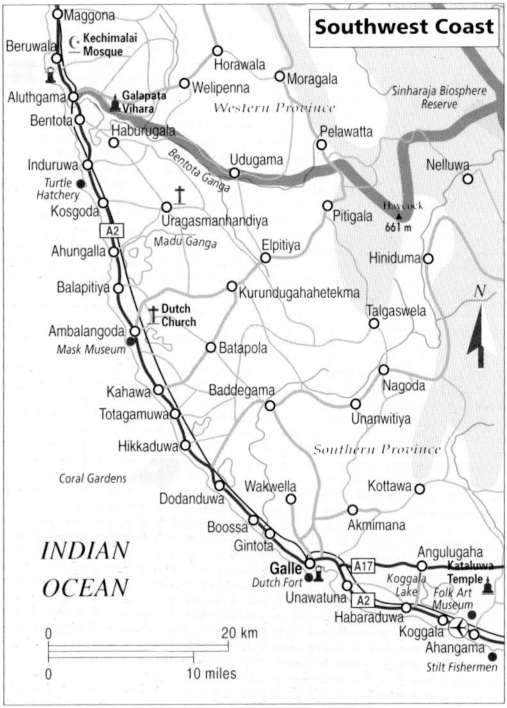

Southwest Coast

KOGGALA

Koggala appears in the
holiday brochures cour-
tesy of its superb beach,
but there is virtually nothing here except for a
handful of all-inclusive
resort hotels. That said, it
has plenty to recommend
it for an idle, undemand-
ing beach holiday.

Kataluwa Temple **

At Kataluwa, 2km (1.2
miles) east of Koggala
beach, this small Buddhist
temple is worth a visit for
its frescoes, said to date
from the 17th century. The
long-nosed, vulpine fea-
tures in European dress are
a less than flattering de-
piction of the Portuguese
merchants who ruled the
region at the time.

WELIGAMA

There isn't much to see at this small fishing port about 30km (20 miles) east of Galle, but the area is known for its **stilt-fishermen**, whose unique style of fishing involves casting their lines from a perch on a sturdy pole 20–50 metres out to sea. Nobody seems to know how or where this unusual technique originated, but it seems to work, as the stilts are passed on from generation to generation and jealously guarded.

SINHARAJA BIOSPHERE RESERVE

This 20km (12-mile) long 'island' of lowland rainforest is 80km (50 miles) northeast of Galle via the A17 highway. It was designated a UNESCO **World Heritage Site** in 1988 and is regarded as one of the most important and bio-diverse conservation areas in Sri Lanka. It has large tracts of undisturbed forest, but sections thinned by selective logging before the area was declared a reserve make it easy to observe endemic bird species including Sri Lanka spurfowl, Sri Lanka jungle fowl, Sri Lanka wood pigeon, Sri Lanka hanging parrot, Sri Lanka grey hornbill, Sri Lanka mynah and Sri Lanka blue magpie, as well as more than 20 others. Mammal species include the giant squirrel and the endemic purple-faced leaf monkey. Also present, but very rarely seen, are leopard.

To gain access to the reserve, visitors must register and pick up a guide at the Kudawa Forest Department office at the entrance to the camp.

Below: *Relaxing on the beach at Unawatuna, which has not yet become overcrowded.*

Galle and the Southwest at a Glance

BEST TIMES TO VISIT

The southwest coast is most pleasant from September to late April. From May to September, when the monsoon kicks in, the beaches may be pounded by heavy seas and sunshine is not guaranteed!

GETTING THERE

By rail: Several services daily between Colombo and Galle, with stops at Alutgama (for Beruwala and Bentota) and Hikkaduwa, and onward travel as far as Matara.
By bus: Frequent services daily along the coastal highway from Colombo to Galle, stopping at Beruwala, Bentota, Ambalangoda and Hikkaduwa. Onward connections to Hambantota and points east, and to Ratnapura and Colombo by the inland route.

GETTING AROUND

Taxis and three-wheelers operate at all resorts, in Galle and other towns. There are frequent buses along the west coast highway, connecting Bentota with Beruwala, Hikkaduwa, Galle and points east.

WHERE TO STAY

Wide range of accommodation available in all resorts, with most luxury and mid-range hotels in Beruwala and Bentota, and largest range of budget accommodation in Hikkaduwa. There is no budget accommodation in Beruwala.

Bentota
LUXURY
Bentota Beach Hotel, National Holiday Resort, Bentota, tel: (034) 75176/7, fax: (034)75179. Four-star hotel with gardens, pool, watersports and view of the sea and Bentota River.

MID-RANGE
Hotel Ceysands, National Holiday Resort, Bentota, tel: (034) 75073, fax: (034) 75395. Two-star hotel with pool, watersports, Bentota River and sea views, beaches and tennis.
Lihinaya Surf Hotel, National Holiday Resort, Bentota, tel: (034) 75126, fax: (034) 75486. Two-star hotel with floodlit pool and tennis courts, scuba centre, deep-sea fishing, watersports.

BUDGET
The Villa, Mohotti Malauwa, tel: (034) 75311, no fax. Comfortable small guesthouse with 14 rooms.

Beruwala
LUXURY
Eden Hotel, Kaluwamodara, Beruwala, tel: (034) 76075, fax: (034) 76181. Five-star, 58-room hotel with 23 deluxe rooms with butler service, four suites, two penthouses, pool, jacuzzi, disco, tennis courts, watersports and marina. The best hotel on the southwest coast.

MID-RANGE
Barberyn Reef Hotel, Morgalla, Beruwala, tel: (034) 76036, fax: (034) 76037. Comfortable hotel, sea views, watersports, tour desk, offers Ayurvedic health cure holidays.

Hikkaduwa
MID-RANGE
Hotel Lanka Supercorals, 390 Galle Road, Hikkaduwa: tel: (09) 77009, fax: (09) 77897. A 100-room hotel, 25 air-conditioned deluxe rooms, garden, pool, TV lounge, kids' corner and pizza restaurant.
Blue Corals Hotel, 332 Galle Road, Hikkaduwa, tel: (09) 77679, fax: (074) 383128. On the beachfront at Hikkaduwa, good value one-star hotel with large pool, beach, garden and two restaurants.

BUDGET
Underwater Safaris, Coral Gardens Hotel, Galle Road, Hikkaduwa, tel: (09) 57023, fax: (09) 57189.
Sunils Beach Hotel, Narigama, Hikkaduwa, tel and fax: (09) 77187. Swimming pool, beach, air-conditioned rooms. Good value.
Reef Beach Hotel, 336 Galle Road, Hikkaduwa, tel: (09) 77197, fax: (074) 383081. Comfortable, good value for money, on the beach.

Galle
LUXURY
Lighthouse Hotel, Dadella, Galle, tel: (09) 23744, fax:

Galle and the Southwest at a Glance

(09) 24021. Exclusive luxury hotel with 60 air-conditioned rooms, large pool, palm-fringed beach and grounds.

MID-RANGE
New Oriental Hotel, 10 Church Street, Galle, tel: (09) 34591, fax: (09) 22059. Sri Lanka's oldest hotel, in historic Dutch colonial building, with pool, four-poster beds in some rooms, atmospheric bar, tropical gardens.

BUDGET
Closenberg Guesthouse, 11 Closenberg Road, Galle, tel and fax: (09) 32241. Comfortable guesthouse in 19th-century colonial building, excellent restaurant.

Ahungalla
LUXURY
Triton Hotel, Ahungalla, tel: (09) 54041, fax: (09) 540456. Superbly luxurious beach resort with huge landscaped pool. On its own beach at Ahungalla, 8km (5 miles) north of Ambalangoda.

Sinharaja Biosphere Reserve
BUDGET
Kudawa Forest Department, bookings (by mail only): Forest Inventory and Management Branch, Forest Department, 82 Rajamalwatta Road, Battaramulla, Colombo 4. Cabins for 2–3 people, dormitory beds and group rooms.

Martin Wijesinghe Guesthouse, Forest View, Kudawa, Veddagala, tel: (045) 5256, offers dormitory beds and rooms with eight beds.

Unawatuna
LUXURY
Unawatuna Beach Resort, Unawatuna, Galle, tel: (09) 32247, fax: (09) 32247. Pool, scuba centre, beach, Ayurvedic health club.

WHERE TO EAT

In addition to restaurants (mostly buffet-style and good value) in resort hotels in Bentota and Beruwala, there are several mid-range restaurants offering western and Sri Lankan dishes, especially in Hikkaduwa, along Galle Road beach and waterfront.

Bentota
MID-RANGE
Haus Athula, 49 Galle Road, Bentota. German speciality restaurant, for a change from curry and noodles.
La Gondola Restaurant, 218 Colombo Road, Bentota. Italian, Chinese and Sri Lankan food.

Hikkaduwa
MID-RANGE
Why Not Rock Café and Beach Restaurant, Galle Road, Narigama, Hikkaduwa. Chinese, Sri Lankan and western dishes, live music, dancing.
Refresh Restaurant, 384 Galle Road, Hikkaduwa.

Sri Lankan and Chinese dishes near Hikkaduwa beachfront.

Galle
MID-RANGE
Closenberg Restaurant, Closenberg Guesthouse (see *Where to Stay*). Sri Lankan and Italian food, excellent bouillabaisse and seafood.

BUDGET
Walkers Tea Centre, 15 Queen Street, Galle. Sample Sri Lankan and Chinese snacks and fine Ceylon tea.
South Ceylon Restaurant, 6 Gamini Mawatha, Galle. Good choice of Sri Lankan specialities.

Ahungalla
MID-RANGE
Lotus Restaurant, Ahungalla. Pleasant restaurant offering a choice of western and Sri Lankan dishes.

TOURS AND EXCURSIONS

Tour operators and travel agencies offer a range of itineraries in combination with beach holidays in the south and southwest, including tours of the ancient cities of Anuradhapura, Polonnaruwa and Sigiriya, Kandy and the hill country, and Ruhuna National Park in the southeast. All mid-range and luxury hotels have tour desks offering a full range of excursions. Scuba diving trips and deep-sea fishing can be arranged by most resort hotels on the southwest coast.

5
The South Coast

East of Galle lie some of Sri Lanka's finest beaches, delightfully unexploited by mainstream tourism but offering enough places to stay to make it an ideal place for a simple, away-from-it-all beach holiday. Spread out along the south coast are small fishing ports like **Matara**, **Tangalla** and **Hambantota**, all of which have retained their own identity and a sleepy charm which as yet has been largely unaffected by major tourism development, though the superb white sand beaches are the equal of – or superior to – any strand on the more popular west coast. Offshore, there are a number of excellent reef and wreck dives.

Inland, there are remarkable, little-visited **temples**, and the region also has some of Sri Lanka's finest wildlife sanctuaries, including the huge **Ruhuna (Yala) National Park** with its herds of wild elephants; the **Bundala National Park**, well-known for its birdlife and crocodile population (and less visited than Yala); the **Debarawewa Wildlife Sanctuary**; and the **Uda Walawe National Park**, where elephants can be seen crossing the Walawe River during the dry season.

All in all, Sri Lanka's south coast is one of the most attractive parts of the island, both for the first-time visitor and for those making a second or third visit to the island. Its array of man-made attractions, ranging from Buddhist and Hindu shrines to Dutch colonial fortresses is complemented by an even more fascinating choice of natural wonders, both along the coast and further inland.

INDIAN OCEAN

Southern Province

Hambantota

Galle •Matara

DON'T MISS

*** **Uda Walawe National Park:** sanctuary for many mammal and bird species.
*** **Bundala National Park:** scrub jungle surrounding large pools attracting birds and marine turtles.
*** **Kataragama:** Sri Lanka's second most sacred place of pilgrimage.
*** **Ruhuna (Yala) National Park:** Sri Lanka's largest and most popular national park.

Opposite: *Dondra Head lighthouse stands at the southern tip of Sri Lanka.*

Above: *The Star Fort at Matara was built in 1763 to guard the river crossing to the main fort.*

MATARA

With around 40,000 inhabitants, Matara is the largest town on the south coast and, as the terminus of the railway line from Colombo, is the gateway to the region. It's a quiet place, though centuries ago it was one of the most important entrepôts for Sri Lanka's **spice** and **gem trade** with the Middle East. It was a strategic port for the Dutch, too, as evidenced by its substantial fortifications.

The oldest part of the town is on a narrow peninsula separated from the mainland by the estuary of the **Nilwala Ganga**, with a good beach on its seaward side. As they did at Galle, the Dutch encircled this easily defended spit of land with sturdy stone walls, which are still in good shape. Within the walls is a charming district of ramshackle old buildings, many of them dating from the Dutch colonial era.

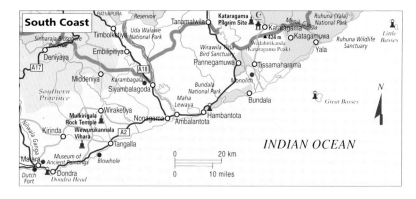

Star Fort and Museum of Ancient Paintings *

On the north bank of the Nilwala Ganga, about 350m (360yd) from the main fort gate, the Dutch built a smaller **outpost fort** in the form of a five-pointed star. Dating from 1763, it was intended to guard the river crossing to the main fort. It now houses a small **museum** of historic paintings and frescoes on wooden panels. Open 09:00–17:00 daily.

Dondra Head *

About 5km (3 miles) east of Matara is Dondra Head, Sri Lanka's southernmost extremity, with a tall **lighthouse** for a landmark and fine views of the coast to either side.

Wewurukannala Temple **

As if to prove that not all Buddhist places of worship are oases of serene elegance and tranquillity, this tacky modern temple 1.5km (1 mile) north of Dikwella village centre on the Beliatta road, slapped onto an unimpressive older building, has to be seen to be believed, with its hundreds of garish life-size models acting out scenes from the life of the Buddha, many-armed devils, monsters and deities, and murals showing the punishments that await sinners in the afterlife (not nice). It looks more like an airport terminal than a temple, and in its courtyard sits what Sri Lankan Buddhists claim is the world's highest **Buddha image**, though there are other colossal Buddha effigies elsewhere in Southeast Asia that also contend for the title. Built out of reinforced concrete in 1966,

> **HOOMANIYA BLOWHOLE**
>
> Claimed to be the second-largest of its kind in the world is the blowhole in the rocky shore at Mawella, 6km (4 miles) east of Dikwella. Wave pressure forces sea water up through a 23m (75ft) crack in the rocks to spout up to 18m (68ft) into the air. It is at its most impressive during the south-west monsoon, in June, when the waves are highest.

Below: *This giant Buddha image at Wewurukannala stands among hundreds of life-size statues acting out scenes from Buddhist myth and legend.*

it's the height of a five-storey building. For a donation to the temple funds, you can climb up inside the gigantic statue and view the countryside around it. Open during daylight hours.

Tangalla ***

The uncrowded small resort of Tangalla, 200km (124 miles) from Colombo, 48km (30 miles) east of Matara, and roughly midway along the south coast, is one of the most pleasant places in the region for a lazy **beach holiday**. Facing east, the village centre straddles a freshwater lagoon where a small river flows into the sea, with a fishing harbour at its mouth. North of the harbour is the long stretch of white sand known as **Medaketiya**. To the south, beyond a low headland, is a series of small sandy coves. There is nothing much to see around here, though there are a few old Dutch houses and a Dutch colonial rest-house in the village, but Tangalla can hardly be beaten for rest and relaxation.

Mulgirigala Rock Temple *

At Mulgirigala, 16km (10 miles) north of Tangalla, this cave temple in a monolithic rock contains reclining Buddha figures in smiling repose as well as standing and seated Buddha figures, surrounded by wall paintings depicting scenes from the life of the Buddha. The rock is crowned by a **Buddhist shrine**. Open daily during daylight hours.

UDA WALAWE NATIONAL PARK

Approximately 32km (20 miles) north of the A2 coastal road, entered via Timbolketiya on the A18 highway to Ratnapura and Colombo, the Uda Walawe National Park was designated in 1972 to offer a refuge to migratory **elephants**, and as wild habitat around it has been lost to cultivation, it has also become a sanctuary for many other mammals, including toque monkey, grey langur, spotted deer, wild pig, leopard and sambar, as well as numerous **birds**. As many as 100 bird species may be spotted here in a single day. Uda Walawe is particularly rich in raptor species, among them white-bellied sea eagle, crested serpent eagle and changeable hawk eagle.

The variety of terrain includes abandoned teak plantation, open grassland and scrub jungle, and this varied habitat makes for an equally rich variety of wildlife and game-spotting opportunities. In the heart of the park is the **Uda Walawe Reservoir**, a huge man-made lake (known in Sri Lanka as a 'tank') with a surface area of up to 3400ha (8401 acres), which provides irrigation for farmlands downstream and generates hydro-electric power.

Uda Walawe is not without its problems; illegal settlement and cattle grazing, especially around the reservoir area, threaten habitat, and relatively large numbers of visitors in their own vehicles also place habitat and animals (especially elephants) under stress. There is also a sporadic poaching problem.

Above: *Spotted deer in Uda Walawe National Park.*
Opposite: *Tangalla is great for a beach holiday.*

WHAT TO WEAR

Beachwear should only be worn at beach resorts; Sri Lankans of all groups are generally modest and find displays of too much skin embarrassing and offensive. Away from the beach, light cotton garments are best, and in the hill country you may want a long-sleeved shirt or wrap after dark when it gets a little cooler.

Above: *Outrigger canoes pulled up out of reach of the surf at Hambantota beach.*

HAMBANTOTA

Heading eastward from Tangalla, the scenery changes from the lush green of the south-west to more open landscapes as you enter the dry zone of southeastern Sri Lanka. Hambantota, 240km (150 miles) from Colombo, is an independent travellers' haven that is showing some of the signs of escalating into a fully fledged holiday resort. Like other south coast towns and villages, it would probably already have made the transition if not for the troubles of the 1980s and 1990s. Hambantota stands on a sandy headland, on the seaward side of which a huge fleet of **outrigger fishing canoes** draws up, and the horizon is almost always dotted with their small triangular sails. With sweeping sandy beaches on either side, it is also a convenient base for exploring the nearby Bundala National Park and, somewhat further away, the Ruhuna National Park and the temples at Kataragama.

Kalametiya **

Just off the main A2 coastal road at the 218km (135-mile) post, this **wetland reserve** – a mixture of mangrove swamp and scrub jungle around two brackish lagoons – is an important location for migrating waterfowl and waders, including four species of plover, curlew, marsh sandpiper, curlew sandpiper, greenshank and yellow wagtail. Residents include three egret species, spoonbills, glossy ibis, purple swamphen and black-winged stilts.

CURRY AND SPICE

Sri Lankans eat curry – vegetable, fish, poultry or meat – for breakfast, dinner and tea. The name comes from *kari*, the Tamil word for spice, and for each dish a different blend of spices is used. Essential ingredients include chilli, ginger, cumin, pepper, turmeric and coriander. Red curry, with plenty of chilli, is the hottest blend, while white curry, using no chilli, is the mildest. Unique to Sri Lanka is black curry, with roasted cumin as the most important flavouring, while in yellow curries turmeric is the key ingredient.

Salt Pans **

Just east of Hambantota a series of salt pans – some still
in use, some disused – attract large numbers of waders
and shore birds, including greater flamingo, spot-billed
pelican, several species of plover and tern, gulls, ducks,
egrets, sandpipers and many others. From west to east
this 16km (10-mile) chain of salt ponds comprises
Karagan Lewaya, lying between Hambantota village and
the mainland; **Maha Lewaya**, a working salt pan on the
main road, easy to spot because of the gleaming piles
of white salt heaped up ready for collection; **Malala
Lewaya, Embilikala Kalapuwa**, and finally **Bundala
Lewaya**, which is regarded as one of Sri Lanka's best
wetland birding sites within the Bundala National Park.

Bundala National Park ***

About 16km (10 miles) east of Hambantota, Bundala is
an accessible expanse of scrub jungle surrounding large
shallow pools which attract many bird species. The
beaches are egg-laying sites for Olive Ridley and

Left: *Hambantota's
salt pans are a magnet for
large flocks of wading birds
and waterfowl.*

Kataragama
Pilgrim Site • •Kataragama
Menik Ganga
Lunuganiwehera
Reservoir
424 m ▲
Wedahitikanda
(Kataragama Peak)
Yala •
Sithulpahuwa
Tissamaharama •
Monolith
Yoda
Wewa
• Bundala

THE MALDIVES

Many tour operators offer holidays which combine a tour of Sri Lanka with a stay on one of the hundreds of coral atolls of the Maldives, the **independent island republic** some 720km (450 miles) southwest of Sri Lanka or one hour's flying time from Colombo. Tourism development has been permitted only on uninhabited atolls to reduce its impact on island society, and there are several luxurious resort islands with comfortable village-style accommodation, superb white sand beaches and excellent scuba diving.

leatherback **turtles**, and hawksbill and green turtles are less frequently seen. Other large reptiles include water monitors and crocodiles, and among the mammal species to be seen within the park boundaries are elephant, spotted deer, grey langur and jackal. Bundala is a relatively small park (compared with the huge expanse of Yala/Ruhuna to the east) but its high concentrations of **mammal** and **bird species** make it one of the best places to see Sri Lanka's abundant wildlife. It is also open all year round, unlike Yala/Ruhuna, which is closed for two to three months in August–October.

Diving **

The **Great Basses** reef, about 40km (25 miles) east of Hambantota, and the **Little Basses**, 80km (50 miles) east, are reputed to offer the best diving in Sri Lanka, with numerous wrecks and many large pelagic fish species to be seen. Both islands are uninhabited and characterized by lighthouses built in the mid-19th century to point out these hazards to shipping. However, very strong currents mean these dive sites are suitable only for extremely experienced divers.

Great Basses and Little Basses have in the past been declared a no-go zone by the security forces, which patrol waters off the east coast to prohibit gun-running to the LTTE guerrillas.

TISSAMAHARAMA

The small town of Tissamaharama is, unsurprisingly, usually just called **Tissa**. About 40km (25 miles) northeast of Hambantota, it is the most convenient jumping-off point for Ruhuna National Park, to the east, and the Kataragama temple complex. Right in the centre of the town is an enormous **tank**, said to have been built some 2300 years ago by the founder of the ancient Sri Lankan kingdom of Ruhuna, **Yatalatissa**, whose capital was here. Also in the centre of town are two large dagobas (Buddhist shrines) attributed to Yatalatissa's heir, **Kavantissa**.

KATARAGAMA

About 80km (50 miles) northeast of Hambantota, Kataragama is Sri Lanka's second most sacred **place of pilgrimage**, rivalling Adam's Peak in its appeal to the devout. Like Adam's Peak, it attracts Sri Lankan Muslims, Buddhists and Hindus in July and August, during the season of pilgrimages and festivals.

The shrine stands among woodland on the banks of a holy river, the **Menik Ganga** (river of jewels), surrounded by seven low, conical hills.

Above: *Hindu pilgrims in procession during the Kataragama Festival.*
Opposite: *Snorkelling is a popular activity on Sri Lanka's south coast.*

MONSOONS

The annual monsoon winds, bringing **heavy rain** and **pounding surf** to Sri Lanka's shores, are caused by temperature and air pressure differentials between the Indian Ocean and the Asian landmass, with prevailing winds sucking warm, humid air off the ocean in summer to cause the southwest monsoon rains.

In winter the prevailing winds shift, and cooler, drier air creates the northeast monsoon, with rains that are not usually as heavy as the southwest monsoon.

Above: *Thousands of pilgrims perform the 'water cutting' ceremony in Kataragama.*

To Buddhists, this forest sanctuary, known as *deviyange kaele* (God's own forest) is where the Lord Buddha planted a sapling of the sacred **bo-tree** of Anuradhapura, sanctifying the spot.

To Hindus, Kataragama is the dwelling place of the Hindu war god **Skanda**, but the deity of Kataragama has many names, among them Kartikeya, Kartikama Murugan, and Kande Yaga.

Both Hindu and Buddhist communities believe that the god of Kataragama has the power to intervene benevolently in their affairs, and thousands visit the shrine each year to appeal for divine aid.

On arrival, pilgrims wash in the cleansing water of the Menik Ganga, crowding the river bank. Each throws a coconut to the stony ground, hoping for it to split auspiciously open – a good omen. Unusually, Hindu and Buddhist pilgrims join in the *perahera* (procession) following the *yantra* (symbol) of the deity as it is paraded from temple to temple.

Temple Complex ***

The temple complex contains a number of Buddhist and Hindu shrines, the most important of which is the unprepossessing **Maha Devala**, a ramshackle brick and concrete building which at first sight gives little hint of any sacred aura. It is said to contain the spear of the multi-visaged, 12-armed warrior deity Skanda, and is visited by Buddhists, Hindus and Muslims.

Other Hindu gods with shrines at Kataragama include **Vishnu**, one of the three supreme Hindu deities, and the chubby, elephant-headed **Ganesha**, the god of prosperity and success and thus, by extension, of business and academia.

The temple complex is known to be very old: the earliest shrine to the resident god is credited to a 2nd century BC local ruler, King Dutugemunu, and the most important Buddhist shrine, the **Kirivehera Dagoba**, was first erected in the 1st century BC.

FIRE-WALKERS

Ceremonies in which priests or pilgrims walk barefoot across a bed of red-hot coals are part of many **Buddhist and Tamil festivals** and in some places are also a tourist attraction. How do they do it? Explanations vary, but the simplest is that red-hot coals are not as hot as they seem, while the calloused skin of people who habitually wear sandals or walk in bare feet give some protection.

Thaipusam Festival

Like some other Tamil Hindu religious events throughout Asia, the annual festival known as Thaipusam – when pilgrims converge on the site from all over Sri Lanka, many of them making the pilgrimage on foot through the hills from Batticaloa on the east coast – seems to have a strong masochistic streak. Devout celebrants allow metal skewers to be driven through their cheeks and tongues, or haul heavy carts carrying symbols and images of the temple deities by cables attached to their backs and

Below: *Fire-walking: a case of calloused feet or deep religious faith?*

ANTIQUES AND SOUVENIRS

Sri Lanka prohibits the export of antiques, which are classified as anything over 50 years old, without special permission. The export of rare books, palm leaf manuscripts and rare works of art and craft works is also banned, as is the export of any wild animal, bird, or reptile or any part of such animals. **Don't**, therefore, **be tempted** by souvenirs made from such materials as ivory, coral, crocodile or snake skin, or turtle-shell.

shoulders by steel hooks. Gory though it appears, it is well attested that the wounds caused by skewers and hooks bleed little – perhaps because large amounts of adrenaline are produced by the body – and heal very quickly. **Fire-walking**, when devotees walk across a bed of glowing coals, is another apparently painful activity from which participants seem to emerge unscathed.

Open all the time; and during *puja* (daily worship) at Maha Devala, at 04:30, 10:30, 18:30. The Kataragama Thaipusam Festival takes place annually over two weeks in July and August; dates can be obtained from the Ceylon Tourist Board information offices in Colombo and overseas (*see* Travel Tips, page 122).

RUHUNA NATIONAL PARK (YALA)

This is Sri Lanka's most popular national park. Easily accessible from Colombo or the A2 coastal highway, the park entrance is approximately 70km (45 miles) east of Hambantota and 30km (19 miles) east of Tissa.

Ruhuna covers almost 1000km² (386 sq miles) of scrub jungle, open savannah, riverine woodland and a long coastline which curves around Sri Lanka's southeast coast. However, only the southwest segment of the park, an area of some 130km² (50 sq miles), is open to visitors.

Ruhuna is the best park in Sri Lanka for spotting **mammals**. However, this is not Africa – the terrain makes animals less easy to spot, and there isn't the density of game you would expect in a national park in East or southern Africa, partly because of the attentions of 19th-century British hunters, who shot thousands of the region's elephant and leopard, and the continuing activity of poachers.

Touring the Park

Elephant get top billing and are what most people come to see, to the extent that joy-riding visitors in jeeps are increasingly driving the animals out of the visitable sector of the park and into its less accessible areas. Other mammals include sloth bear, spotted deer, mouse deer, barking deer, sambur, grey langur, toque monkey, wild boar, and smaller species including stripe-necked and ruddy mongoose and jackal. Both marsh and estuarine crocodiles may be seen, and a day's birding can record as many as 100 species, among them such rarities as red-faced malkoha, great thick-knee, sirkeer malkoha, blue-faced malkoha and painted stork.

Access is by vehicle only, and **four-wheel drive** is required. Ruhuna is usually closed from late August to mid-October. The best time to be sure of seeing the maximum is during the dry season, when animals cluster around water sources in multi-species groups. You may see elephant, wild pig, deer, monkeys and even the elusive pangolin drinking from the same pool, along with conspicuously colourful peacock and jungle fowl.

Above: *Elephants can be seen in large numbers in Ruhuna National Park.*

WILDLIFE

Loss of habitat to farmland, poaching and trapping have put pressure on Sri Lanka's wildlife, with larger species such as leopard and elephant confined to wildlife reserves. That said, a total of more than 2 million hectares (4,942,000 acres) is now set aside in protected areas including national parks, sanctuaries, natural parks and forest reserves, and the in-built Buddhist injunction to respect all living things also provides Sri Lanka's endemic species with some protection.

The South Coast at a Glance

September to late April is the best time to visit the south coast. The **monsoon season** affects this area from May to September, making the seas rough and reducing the chances of sunshine.

By rail: The main coastal railway line from Colombo connects Galle and the south coast as far as Matara with all east coast towns and resorts. Journey time to Matara is around 6 hours.
By road: Buses connect Colombo and east coast towns with Galle, Matara, Hambantota and points between, along the A2 coastal highway; journey time is 4 hours. From Hambantota, buses operate to Nuwara Eliya and Kandy. Buses also connect Colombo and Ratnapura with Hambantota via the inland A4–A18 route, with a journey time of about 4 hours. There are three-wheelers and taxis in Hambantota and other main villages such as Dikwella, Tangalla and Tissamaharama. At Matara, bullock-drawn carriages with lumpy red upholstery are still an everyday form of public transport, and rather a novelty for any tourist! Moving at no more than walking pace, they are a great way to tour around the old town.

The best option is a three-wheeler or a taxi, readily available in the main villages. Matara has an interesting option: bullock-drawn carriages with red upholstery.

Uda Walawe National Park: hire a four-wheel drive vehicle and driver from Nilan Safari, P6 Tanamalwila Road, Uda Walawe, tel: (047) 33300, or from the Centauria Tourist Hotel, Embelipitiya, tel: (047) 30104.
Bundala National Park: jeeps and drivers for hire from guesthouses and hotels in Hambantota.
Ruhuna National Park: jeeps can be hired with driver in Tissamaharama town centre, or from Yala Safari Beach Hotel or Brown's Safari Beach Motel, tel: (047) 20326, fax: (047) 43375.

Luxury resort hotels such as those on the west coast and in Colombo are thin on the ground along the south coast. However, there are plenty of comfortable mid-range hotels and smaller family-run guesthouses in towns and beach villages including Matara, Tangalla, Hambantota and Tissamaharama, and at the villages close to the region's national parks, offering good accommodation.

Matara
MID-RANGE
Polhena Reef Garden Hotel, 30 Beach Road, Polhena, Matara, tel: (041) 22478. Affordable, simple mid-range hotel.
BUDGET
Paradise Beach Club, 140 Gunasiri Mahomi Mawatha, Mirissa, tel: (071) 24665, no fax. Small, family-run beach hotel just outside Matara.

Tangalla
LUXURY
Club Dikwella Village, for reservations/information contact Connaissance de Ceyland Ltd., 58 Dudley Senanayake Mawatha, Colombo 8, tel: (01) 685601, fax: (01) 685555. The most luxurious hotel in the area, on a palm-fringed promontory with beaches on two sides and a fine pool.

MID-RANGE
Dikwella Relais Club, Matara Road, Dikwella, tel: (041) 2941, no fax. Resort hotel with emphasis on sports and activities including scuba, windsurfing and tennis.
Dikwella Beach Hotel, 112 Mahawela Road, Dikwella, tel: (041) 55271, fax: (041) 55410. Comfortable beach hotel.
Tangalla Bay Beach Hotel, Pallikudawa, Tangalla, tel: (047) 40346, no fax. Adequate mid-range hotel, a bit bland in its decor.

The South Coast at a Glance

BUDGET

Namal Garden Tourist Guesthouse, 58/3 Madaketiya Road, Tangalla, tel: (047) 40532, no fax. Small and comfortable guesthouse.

Hambantota
MID-RANGE

Peacock Beach Hotel, Galle Road, Hambantota, tel/fax: (047) 20377. Probably the best hotel in the Hambantota area, 80 rooms, good swimming pool.

Hotel Oasis, Sisilasagama, Hambantota, tel: (047) 20650, fax: (047) 20651. Comfortable tourist hotel with good location.

Tissamaharama
MID-RANGE

Tissamaharama Rest House, Tissamaharama, tel: (047) 37299, fax: (047) 37201. Best place to stay in Tissa, pool, some rooms with lake view, good restaurant.

BUDGET

Priyankara Tour Inn, Kataragama Road, Tissamaharama, tel: (047) 37206. Simple budget guesthouse in central Tissa.

NATIONAL PARKS
Uda Walawe National Park
BUDGET

Centauria Tourist Hotel, New Town, Embelipitiya, tel: (047) 30104. Basic small guesthouse close to the park entrance, clean and friendly.

Ruhuna National Park
MID-RANGE

Yala Safari Beach Hotel, Yala, Tissamaharama, tel: (047) 20471. This hotel is operated by leading Sri Lankan chain Jetwing Hotels, 46/26 Nawam Mawatha, Colombo 2, tel: (01) 345700, fax: (01) 345729. A comfortable hotel at the sea, next to the park entrance. It is the best place to stay in order to explore Ruhuna. The hotel can also organize various safaris.

Brown's Safari Beach Motel, Yala, Tissamaharama, tel: (047) 20326, fax: (047) 43375. Part of the Aitken Spence hotel group, also on the beach at the park entrance, and can organize various safaris.

WHERE TO EAT

All the small towns and villages of the south coast and its hinterland have their complement of small family-run restaurants serving curries and other Sri Lankan basics, and sometimes the Sri Lankan version of Chinese rice and noodle dishes such as chow mein and chop suey. Small roadside food stalls pop up at strategic locations (usually around markets, bus stations or along the waterfront of each village) in the evening. However, this is not an area that has seen much tourism development, and familiar European and international dishes are not widely found outside the restaurants of mid-range holiday hotels. There are no outstanding restaurants in the area that truly warrant special recommendation.

TOURS AND EXCURSIONS

Trips to the national parks of the south with your own four-wheel drive vehicle and driver can easily be organized on the spot in Hambantota or Tissamaharama, where local drivers actively tout for business at the bus stations and guesthouses. Most hotels and guesthouses will help to arrange vehicles and drivers, and also provide meals to take with you. Cost is a matter for negotiation and you should make a firm agreement on the price before leaving, specifying exactly what you will and won't pay for.

More professionally organized visits to the national parks of the south can be arranged through several Colombo-based companies and tour companies specializing in birding and ecotourism. These include:

A Baur & Co, Wildlife and Birdwatching Service, PO Box 11, Colombo 1, tel: (01) 320551, fax: (01) 448493.

Adventurers Lanka, 12A Simon Mewavitharana Road, Colombo 3, tel: (01) 576474, fax: (01) 575425.

6
Anuradhapura and the North West

Sri Lanka's northwest, also known as the dry zone and more recently dubbed the country's '**Cultural Triangle**', is a world apart from the busy city streets of Colombo or the beach resorts of the south and west coasts. Compared with the lush greenery of the tea-growing hill country around Kandy, this rolling, open country is **arid**, coloured in shades of dusty brown earth and golden ripening **rice fields**. Farming here depends on artificial irrigation, and the countryside is dotted with artificial reservoirs to hold rainwater and allow crops to thrive through the dry season.

The region contains some of Sri Lanka's most awe-inspiring sights, including temples and fortresses crowning steep rock pinnacles like **Sigiriya** that rise above the dusty plains, and the ruins of lost ancient cities like **Anuradhapura** and **Polonnaruwa** – the capitals of sophisticated civilizations which toppled and vanished from history centuries ago, and were rediscovered only in the 19th century. Huge rock-cut Buddha images, dagobas and cave temples testify to a very ancient Buddhist tradition.

According to the *Mahavansa*, the epic genealogy of the Sri Lankan kings from the 6th century BC until the mid-18th century, Anuradhapura was founded in 457BC by the mighty King Pandukhabaya. Although the rulers of this remarkable nation never managed to extend their reign over the whole of Sri Lanka, they dominated the island for more than a thousand years, and Anuradhapura was famed throughout Asia for the excel-

INDIAN OCEAN

Anuradhapura · North Central Province
Puttalam
North Western Province · Polonnaruwa
Kurunegala

DON'T MISS

*** Anuradhapura: ruined capital of Sri Lanka's greatest kingdom, rediscovered in the 19th century.
*** Polonnaruwa: thousand-year-old ruined imperial city.
*** Sigiriya: dizzy cliff-top citadel with superb views and 1700-year-old rock paintings.
** Dambulla: cliffside cave temple with dozens of Buddha images.

Opposite: *The reclining and standing rock-carved Buddhas at the Gal Vihara.*

CULTURAL TRIANGLE

Sri Lanka's 'cultural triangle' includes Kandy, Anuradhapura, Polonnaruwa as well as Sigiriya. If you plan to visit all of these, you can make **substantial savings** (around 40 per cent of the cost of buying each ticket separately) on entry costs by buying a triangle ticket which entitles you to one visit to each site, over a period of two weeks from first use. The tickets are on sale at ticket offices in Anuradhapura, Sigiriya, Polonnaruwa and Kandy, and at the time of writing cost US$37.50.

lence of its temple art and palace architecture, the ingenuity and skill of its irrigation engineers, and its military prowess. It was through the kings of Anuradhapura, too, that Buddhism came to Sri Lanka, from the court of the great Murya Emperor of India, Ashok, who sent envoys to the Hindu ruler of Anuradhapura, Devanampiya Tissa (247–207BC), to persuade him to convert to the **Buddhist faith**.

Buddhist or not, the Sinhalese kings and princes of the Lankan kingdoms fought among themselves almost continuously, sons plotting against fathers and brothers against brothers, in a never-ending power struggle that weakened their kingdoms and often left them open to attack by Tamil invaders from southern India.

As well as its fascinating ancient sites, the northwest also has some fine and completely undeveloped **beaches**, scuba diving in the little-visited coastal lagoon, and Sri Lanka's largest National Park, **Wilpattu**.

Many of the most important sights of the northwest are distributed along or close to the main A9 highway, with a detour east to Sigiriya and Polonnaruwa on the A6/A11 road. You can therefore choose to head straight for Anuradhapura, then travel back stopping off at other places, or as most people do, stop off at each location on the way north, with Anuradhapura, the most impressive of all the region's sights – and perhaps the most striking in all Sri Lanka – as a climax to your journey.

In view of the troubled security situation in northern Sri Lanka, you are strongly recommended not to travel north of Vavuniya, situated 53km (35 miles) north of Anuradhapura on the A9. There are frequent military checkpoints on this route, and those without military passes are likely to be refused permission to travel in view of continued guerrilla activity by the LTTE.

DAMBULLA

The gateway to the northwest, and the first of its great sights, is Dambulla, where one of Sri Lanka's finest **cave temples** stands – 150m (150yd) outside the modern village, and 72km (45 miles) north of Kandy on the

> ### HABARANA
>
> Although it is of no great interest in itself, the small town of Habarana is the most **convenient base** for exploring Dambulla and Sigiriya, with a choice of mid-range and budget accommodation and a handful of simple restaurants.

Opposite: *The quadrangle complex at Anuradhapura encloses a rich collection of ancient buildings.*

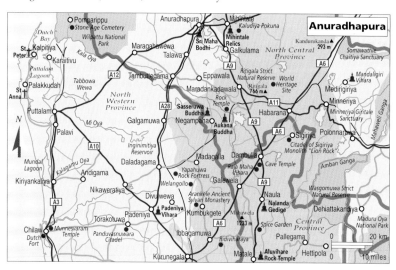

outskirts of the dry zone. Within five large caverns – the largest some 50m (360ft) deep and 6m (19ft) in height, are sitting, standing and reclining Buddha images by the dozen, as well as Hindu gods; and each cave is decorated with mural paintings of **scenes from the Buddha's life**. These murals are much more modern than the carvings, some of which are as much as 200 years old. The first temples are said to have been created by King Valagam Bahu (104–76BC), one of the kings of Anuradhapura, who was driven from his throne by South Indian invaders during the 1st century BC. He took shelter here, and on regaining power had a rock temple built in thanksgiving. The ascent to the caves – which are on the higher part of one of the smooth, sloping crags of rock that are a feature of dry zone landscapes – is steep, but as a reward for your efforts there is a great view of the crag of Sigiriya, about 20km (12 miles) away. Open daily 06:00–19:00.

SIGIRIYA

Opposite: *The Sigiriya rock fortress rises high above the flat plains of the dry zone.*

Making the most of Sigiriya requires a good head for heights, as the last part of the way to the top of this 200m (656ft) plug of rock, fortified in the late 5th century AD, is a scramble over a series of shallow steps with a sheer drop on one side. Around the monolithic crag are the ramparts of the lower citadel, enclosing a complex of ruined miniature summer palaces and royal swimming pools.

Palace Complex ★★★

The palace complex and clifftop citadel were built in around AD473–480 by Kasyapa, a patricidal usurper of the throne of Anuradhapura, as a bulwark against attack by his half-brother Mogallana, the rightful heir to the throne. Instead of staying behind his walls when Mogallana finally launched his bid for the throne in AD491, however, Kasyapa went out to fight, was defeated and committed suicide. Mogallana was crowned king in AD495 and returned the throne to Anuradhapura, where he reigned for the next 18 years. Sigiriya was gradually abandoned and fell into disuse, and its treasures were not rediscovered until the 19th century.

Midway up the stairway are the Sigiriya Damsels, the only **secular art** to have survived from the early Sinhalese kingdoms. In Kasyapa's time, the rock wall was graced by hundreds of sensuous paintings of skimpily clad court beauties, but only 22 have survived the ravages of time, weather and vandalism. A little further along, the Mirror Wall preserves hundreds of graffiti dating from as early as the 8th century and providing linguists with vital insight into the evolution of the written and oral Sinhalese language. The final section of the stair originally passed between the paws of a colossal brickwork lion which formed a gateway into the upper citadel and gave the rock its name, which in Sinhala means 'lion rock'.

There is little left of the palace of Kasyapa except for his rock-cut throne and a large stone pool, probably a reservoir, cut out of the rock. The view, however, is absolutely breathtaking.

THE LION KING

The semi-legendary **King Vijaya** (543–505BC) is regarded by the Sinhalese as the first king of Sri Lanka and the **forefather** of their race. Vijaya was said to be descended from a princess of the Kalinga kingdom of Bengal, who mated with a lion to produce a twin son and daughter, Sinhabahu and Sinhabvali, from whose marriage Vijaya was born. Exiled from his father's kingdom, Vijaya reached Sri Lanka, where he married first a demon princess, Kuveni, then a human princess from southern India, and founded the line of Sinhalese kings.

Above: *Elaborate carvings adorn the steps of the Image House at Polonnaruwa.*
Below: *It seems hard to believe that Topa Wewa (Parakrama Samudra) is a man-made lake.*

POLONNARUWA

Deciding which of the two ancient capitals – Polonnaruwa or Anuradhapura – is the more impressive is a tough call. Anuradhapura is much older and its ruins cover a greater expanse of land. Polonnaruwa is much more recent – although it was built more than a millennium ago – and is also better preserved.

Ancient City ★★★

Just north of present-day Polonnaruwa town, 140km (90 miles) north of Kandy, are the ruins of ancient Polonnaruwa, which date from the late 10th century, when the Chola kings of southern India invaded Sri Lanka and conquered Anuradhapura. The invaders moved their capital to Polonnaruwa, strategically located for defence against attacks from the unconquered Sinhala kingdom of Ruhuna, in the southeast (which has lent its name to Sri Lanka's most visited national park, *see* page 86). Their defences ultimately proved inadequate and in 1070 they were forcibly evicted from Polonnaruwa by the Sinhalese ruler Vijayabahu I. Recognizing, however, that Anuradhapura's location made it vulnerable to any assault from southern India, he and his successors made their capital at Polonnaruwa, adding enormous temples, palaces, parks, gardens and huge tanks. By the 13th century AD, however, new waves of attacks from southern India forced the Sinhalese kings to abandon the north of the island, and the kingdoms of Kotte in the southwest (near modern Colombo), and Kandy, in the highlands, became the centres of Sinhalese power.

The ruins of the ancient city stand on the east shore of a large artificial lake, the Topa Wewa Lake, or Parakrama Samudra (the Sea of Parakrama), created by King Parakramabahu I (1153–86), whose reign was Polonnaruwa's golden age. Within a rectangle of city walls stand palace buildings and clusters of dozens of dagobas, temples and various other religious buildings.

A scattering of other historic buildings can be found to the north of the main complex, outside the city walls and close to the main road to Habarana and Dambulla. To see many of the relics excavated from the site – such as the stone lion which once

SERENDIPITY

The English writer **Horace Walpole** (1717–97) coined the word serendipity – meaning '**the art of making lucky discoveries**' – in 1754. He was inspired by one of the tales of the *Arabian Nights*, 'The Three Princes of Serendib', whose leading characters are constantly making accidental discoveries of things they are not seeking.

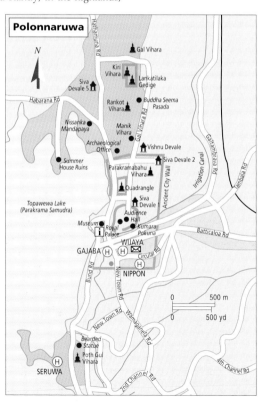

Polonnaruwa

N

Gal Vihara
Kiri Vihara
Lankatilaka Gedige
Siva Devale 5
Rankot Vihara
Buddha Seema Pasada
Habarana Rd
Hathamuna Rd
Gal Vihara Rd
Nissanka Mandapaya
Manik Vihara
Archaeological Office
Vishnu Devale
Summer House Ruins
Parakramabahu Vihara
Siva Devale 2
Ancient City Wall
Irrigation Canal
Gatambrava Rd
Tambala Rd
Quadrangle
Siva Devale 1
Topawewa Lake (Parakrama Samudra)
Audience Hall
Museum
Royal Palace
Kumara Pokuna
Batticaloa Rd
WIJAYA
GAJABA
Circular Rd
NIPPON
Rd Pung
New Town Rd
Wamaganela Rd
0   500 m
0   500 yd
Bearded Statue
Poth Gul Vihara
SERUWA
2nd Channel Rd
4th Channel Rd

AYURVEDIC MEDICINE

Ayurvedic therapies, which
are said to have originated in
India thousands of years ago,
are offered at several of Sri
Lanka's luxury resort hotels.
The Ayurveda (from the Hindi
ayur: life and *veda:* knowledge) stresses a **holistic
approach to health**, elim-
inating toxins from the body
through massage, sauna
and diet which is intended to
strengthen the *prana*, or life
force, coupled with *bhavana*,
or meditation, to achieve
peace of mind.

Below: *The Vatadage at
Polonnaruwa houses four
Buddha images.*

guarded the palace of King Nissanka Malla, or the fine
Hindu bronzes unearthed from the ruins of the Siva
Devale Temple – you may have to visit the **National
Museum in Colombo**, where they are kept. However,
with the opening of the new Polonnaruwa Visitor
Information Centre and its museum in 1998/9 some of
the key exhibits were scheduled to return to the place
where they were discovered.

Polonnaruwa Visitor Information Centre and Museum ***

Built with the help of the Dutch government, this centre,
on the banks of the lake, uses designer displays, detailed
descriptive texts and a five-minute video presentation to
complement its collection of archaeological finds. With a
huge **scale model** of the site, it brings Polonnaruwa's
palaces and temples to life, and it is well worth visiting
before you set out to explore the complex. Opening
hours are the same as for the rest of the site, see page 99.

The Royal Palace ***

In the centre of the complex stood the Royal Palace, built by Parakramabahu I and originally a massive wood and stone structure seven storeys in height, with a floor plan of 31m by 13m (100ft by 43ft). The upper floors were of wood, and only the massive, 3m (10ft) thick lower walls survive.

Above: *Audience Hall of the Royal Palace, where the kings of Polonnaruwa met emissaries of other nations.*

Immediately to the east of the Palace stands the Audience Hall, used by the kings of Polonnaruwa to hear petitions from the nobles of the kingdom and to meet emissaries from foreign rulers. Superb stone lions seated at the top of the steps leading into the hall were symbols of royal power, as were the elephants which form a frieze around the lower part of the outer wall. Next to the Audience Hall is the Kumara Pokuna (Royal Bathing Pool) which was fed with water from the stream which runs through the palace grounds.

Nissanka Malla's Palace **

Standing close to the shore of the lake, the ruins of the palace of Parakramabahu I's successor, Nissanka Malla (1187–96), are less well preserved than those of the Royal Palace, but are attractively located. This palace group includes a royal bathing pool just south of the palace, and the King's Council Chamber, where the names of the king's ministers can be seen carved into the pillars which supported the chamber roof.

Siva Devale **

Immediately north of the Royal Palace complex is the Siva Devale, a 13th-century Hindu temple dating from the period of south Indian conquest that followed the final decline of Sinhalese power in the north of the

---

BUDDHIST ARCHITECTURE

Three styles of religious building appear frequently in the ruined cities. Most common is the **dagoba**, a bell-like stone or brick building surmounted by a pointed spire and containing a relic of the Buddha in a small central chamber. **Gedige temples** like those at Polonnaruwa have massive walls and corbelled roofs, while the **vatadage**, a circular relic house with doorways to the north, south, east and west, is unique to Sri Lanka. Because of the thickness of the walls, all of these seem much smaller inside than out. The entire Polonnaruwa Complex is open from 08:00–18:00; the last tickets are sold at 17:00.

Above: *The Stone Book records achievements of King Nissanka Malla.*

MOONSTONES

A distinctive decorative motif that occurs frequently in ancient Sri Lankan Buddhist architecture is the so-called moonstone – a semi-circular bottom step or doorstep decorated with a stylized half-lotus flower expanding in rings which are intricately adorned with carvings of birds, leaves and flowers, and the four symbolic beasts – lions, elephants, horses and bulls – within an outer ring of stylized flames.

---

island. The technical skills of its masons are evident from the fine, precisely cut stonework of its walls. The brick-domed roof, however, has not survived. There are several Siva Devales (Shiva Temples) at Polonnaruwa, reflecting the popularity of this powerful member of Hinduism's ruling trinity of deities.

Quadrangle ***

A few yards northwest of the Siva Devale, the complex known as the Quadrangle stands within its own rectangle of walls, guarding the richest collection of ancient buildings in any of Sri Lanka's ruined capitals. In the southeast corner of the Quadrangle stands the Vatadage (reliquary), a circular building some 18m (59ft) in diameter, with four entrances leading to a central dagoba (shrine) which houses four seated Buddha images.

Clockwise around this building, from the southwest corner of the Quadrangle, is the **Thuparama**, a fine example of the gedige style of temple architecture which flourished at Polonnaruwa, and the only one to survive with its roof still in place.

West of the Vatadage is the **Latha Mandapaya**, a miniature dagoba encircled by stone columns topped with carved lotus buds, and surrounded by a carved stone trellis. Beyond this is the **Atadage**, the ruin of a tooth relic shrine built during the reign of Vijayabahu I. Next to it is a cluster of small Hindu shrines.

Immediately north of the Vatadage is the **Hatadage**, another tooth reliquary building which was constructed in the reign of Nissanka Malla, and to the east of this stands the **Gal Pota**, or Stone Book, a 9m (29ft) stone carving of one of the palm leaf books used to record Buddhist texts and royal genealogies. The inscriptions on it boast of the achievements of King Nissanka Malla, a man who seems to have been acutely aware of the long shadow cast by his great father, whose achievements he constantly sought to equal and outdo.

Finally, in the northeast corner of the Quadrangle, stands the **Satmahal Prasada**, a six-storey, pagoda-like building which is unlike anything else in Sri Lanka, and has left archaeologists stymied as to its origin.

Still within the perimeter of the city walls, north of the Quadrangle complex, are three more devales, including a **Siva Devale** to the west of the road, and on the opposite side of the road a **Vishnu Devale** and yet another **Siva Devale**, a stone temple which is the oldest surviving building at Polonnaruwa. South of it looms the **Parakramabahu Vihara**, one of the largest dagobas in Polonnaruwa.

> **TEN SRI LANKAN PROVERBS**
>
> 'Ambition begets vexations' (Sinhalese)
>
> 'Eat coconuts while you have teeth' (Sinhalese)
>
> 'Even the fall of a dancer is a somersault' (Sinhalese)
>
> 'What you do to others will bear fruit in you' (Sinhalese)
>
> 'By committing foolish acts, one learns wisdom' (Sinhalese)
>
> 'Even monks of the same temple quarrel sometimes' (Sinhalese)
>
> 'As individuals go their own way, destiny accompanies them' (Tamil)
>
> 'The one who teaches is the giver of eyes' (Tamil)
>
> 'Our shadow will follow us' (Tamil)
>
> 'Kind words conquer' (Tamil)

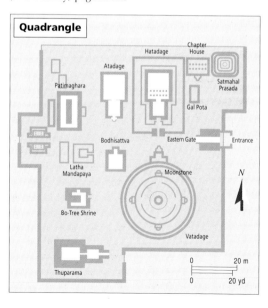

Quadrangle

MUDRAS

The hands of each Buddha image are shown in the various *mudras*. These are gestures, or hand positions, with a range of **symbolic meanings**. In the *adhaya mudra*, the right hand of the image is raised to symbolize protection. In the *vitarka mudra*, the index finger touches the thumb, symbolizing teaching and wisdom, while in the meditative *dhyana mudra* the hands are cupped and resting in the figure's lap.

Below: *The huge Lankatilaka Gedige, carved with elaborate friezes, was built by King Parakramabahu.*

Alahana Pirivena Complex **

North of the city walls, and scattered close to the roadside over a distance of some 6km (4 miles) from the main site, are several striking buildings, some of which are in the process of restoration. From south to north, these are:

Rankot Vihara

The largest dagoba in Polonnaruwa at 55m (180ft) high, this building is the hub of the group of buildings known as the Alahana Pirivena ('CremACY College') group which formed part of a monastic college during the reign of Parakramabahu.

Buddha Seema Pasada

A conspicuous landmark, this is the tallest of the buildings north of the city walls and was the meeting hall of the chief abbot of the monastery complex.

Lankatilaka Gedige

A huge temple built during the reign of Parakramabahu, the 17m (56ft) high walls still stand, but the roof is gone, as is the head of the colossal Buddha image that stands within. The walls are carved with friezes of Polonnaruwa in its golden age.

Kiri ('White') Vihara

Aptly named, this large dagoba's whitewashed plaster has survived seven centuries of abandonment to the jungle between the collapse of the Polonnaruwa kingdom and its rediscovery in the 19th century. It is the best preserved of the island's unrestored dagobas.

Gal Vihara

Also known as the Cave of the Spirits of Knowledge, this is one of the most important Buddhist shrines. It takes the form of three colossal Buddha images carved out of a granite cliff. Most prominent is the standing image, 7m (23ft) tall, which was at one time thought to represent Ananda, the Buddha's first disciple, but is now regarded as being a Buddha image like the others. Next to it is an enormous 14m (46ft) reclining Buddha. Two smaller, less skillfully carved Buddha images occupy niches in the rock nearby.

Demala Maha Seya

Abandoned before completion, this large mound is what remains of Parakramabahu's grandiose bid to build the largest dagoba in the Buddhist world. He died before the work was completed.

Above: *Serene Buddha image at the Gal Vihara, one of the most important Buddhist shrines.*

PARAKRAMABAHU

Parakramabahu the Great (1153–86) defeated several rival princes to be crowned king, first of Polonnaruwa and the surrounding region of Rajarata, then in 1155 of all Sri Lanka. His reign was the golden age of Polonnaruwa, and with the building of the great reservoir that bore his name, the Sea of Parakrama, the artificial irrigation system reached its peak. But his achievements and adventures abroad – when he invaded kingdoms in southern India, Burma and Thailand – drained the kingdom's resources and within two decades of his death his empire fell apart.

Above: *Fearsome looking masks symbolize benign naga (cobra) spirits.*
Opposite: *Anuradhapura stands among huge man-made lakes that are more than 1600 years old.*

NAGAS

Proving that not all cultures regard the **serpent** as the emblem of evil, the *nagas* of Sri Lanka and India are benevolent cobra spirits which, according to Hindu and Buddhist belief, bring prosperity, good fortune, marriage and fertility to their worshippers. *Nagas* are a common theme of religious art, and *naga* masks, depicting them as grinning, long-toothed, pop-eyed beings, are popular souvenirs.

OFF THE BEATEN TRACK

Between Polonnaruwa and Anuradhapura are several ancient religious sites which are well worth a visit.

Medirigiriya *

About 30km (20 miles) north of Polonnaruwa, the attraction of this out-of-the-way village is the 1300-year-old temple site of **Mandaligiri Vihara**. The circular relic temple here, dating from the 8th century AD, is similar in architectural style to the Vatadage at Polonnaruwa, with concentric rings of columns and seated Buddha images facing north, south, east and west. It stands on a hillock just outside the village and is signposted. Open daily during daylight hours.

Ritigala ***

Remarkably few people seem to visit Ritigala. This archaeological site is, however, scheduled for UNESCO listing as a **World Heritage Site**. About 23km (15 miles) west of Habarana, off the main A11 highway, it can conveniently be visited on the way from Polonnaruwa to Anuradhapura. The main cultural attraction is the **Ritigala Forest Monastery**, with **superb views** over the entire zone from the wooded slopes of the region's highest range of hills, rising to 600m (1969ft). The 6.5km (4-mile) range of hills is also rich in endangered bird species, including black eagle, grey hornbill, Sri Lanka spurfowl, Malabar pied hornbill and spot-winged thrush. Mammals, including sloth bear, leopard and elephant, have been seen, but are shy. The monastery and reserve are open daily, 08:00–18:00, last entry 17:00.

Mihintale *

About 13km (8 miles) east of the main Anuradhapura complex, Mihintale is a rock sanctuary which dates from at least 250BC and still attracts its share of Buddhist pilgrims as well as tourists. Below are the ruins of a hospice and almshouse built more than 2200 years ago and surrounded by gigantic shade trees. There's a fairly stiff climb up more than 100 steps to the **Ambasthala Dagoba**, a centuries-old Buddhist shrine, and at the summit of the rock is the smaller **Hirigaduseya Dagoba**. From here, there is an excellent view of the whole Anuradhapura site. Other features of Mihintale include 60 to 70 small caves used in the past as places of meditation by Buddhist monks.

POSON FULL MOON

The *Poson* Full Moon Festival **commemorates the arrival of Buddhism** in Sri Lanka in the 3rd century BC and centres on the huge dagoba at Mihintale, where Mahindra, son of the great Indian Buddhist Emperor Ashok, first taught the Buddhist faith to the people of Anuradhapura. There are also religious festivals and processions elsewhere around the island.

ANURADHAPURA

The largest and oldest of all Sri Lanka's ancient cities, Anuradhapura is a fitting climax to any tour of the Cultural Triangle. Arguably, it takes a bit more effort to imagine it as it was more than 2000 years ago, with palaces and huge dagobas standing up to nine storeys high, a main processional avenue 24km (16 miles) long, and the richly decorated, ostentatious mansions of Sinhalese nobles and wealthy foreign merchants.

Opposite: *The sacred bo- or bodhi tree at Anuradhapura is said to be the oldest tree in the world.*

Founded by King Pandukhabaya in 437BC, by the mid-3rd century BC Anuradhapura's fame had spread as far as the Roman-Hellenistic world of the Mediterranean and by the 1st century AD it had established trade and diplomatic links with China. The Jetavana treasures, unearthed over the past 20 years (some are now displayed in the partially completed Jetavanarama Museum, on site) show evidence of these links to east and west.

Anuradhapura was the royal seat of more than 250 Buddhist and Hindu kings recorded in the royal genealogies, and the pre-eminent city on the island for some 1400 years.

Anuradhapura's proximity to southern India both enriched it and encouraged the kingdom's conversion to Buddhism, but was also its eventual downfall, making it vulnerable to the invading Tamil forces of Rajaraja Chola, who sacked the city in the 11th century AD. The Sinhalese capital then moved to Polonnaruwa. Although attempts were made to preserve its monuments after the overthrow and expulsion of the Chola dynasty, it was never restored to its former glory.

The Mawathu Oya River forms the boundary

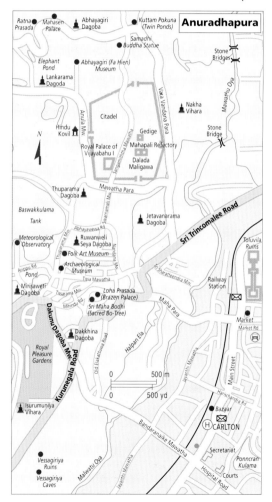

Anuradhapura

Ratna Prasada · Mahasen Palace · Abhayagiri Dagoba · Kuttam Pokuna (Twin Ponds) · Samadhi Buddha Statue · Stone Bridges · Elephant Pond · Abhayagiri (Fa Hien) Museum · Lankarama Dagoda · Mawathu Oya · Anula Mw · Citadel · Nakha Vihara · Hindu Kovil · Gedige · Stone Bridge · N · Royal Palace of Vijayabahu I · Mahapali Refectory · Dalada Maligawa · Vaka Vandana Para · Saggalmatta Mawatha · Thuparama Dagoba · Mawatha Para · Baswakkulama Tank · Jetavanarama Dagoba · Sri Trincomalee Road · Meteorological Observatory · Ruwanweli Seya Dagoba · Abhayawewa Mw · Folk Art Museum · Toluvila Ruins · Archaeological Museum · Anippu Rd · Pond · Tissa Mawatha · Railway Station · Mirisaweti Dagoba · Loha Prasada (Brazen Palace) · Tissarama Mw · Mihindu Rd · Sri Maha Bodhi (Sacred Bo-Tree) · Maha Para · Market · Market Rd · Dakkhina Dagoba · Dakunu Dagoba Mw · Royal Pleasure Gardens · Hajpan Ela · Old Elakattuwa Road · Kurunegala Road · Main Street · 0　500 m · 0　500 yd · Isurumuniya Vihara · Jayanti Mawatha · Herschandra Rd · Bazaar · Bandaranaike Mawatha · CARLTON · Vessagiriya Ruins · Vessagiriya Caves · Malwatu Oya · Secretariat · Ponncran Kulama · Hospital Road · Courts

between the sacred ancient city and the modern town of Anuradhapura, east of the river. To the west are several large tanks, some of them the work of King Mahasena (AD276–303), whose passion for large-scale construction also endowed the city with the enormous Jetavanarama Dagoba.

As at Polonnaruwa, Anuradhapura's secular buildings were built partly or entirely of wood, which has not survived the centuries, whereas the giant dagobas, made entirely of earth, brick and stone, still stand complete. All sites and museums within the sacred city complex of Anuradhapura are open 08:00–17:00 daily.

Sri Maha Bodhi (Sacred Bo-Tree) **

Said to be the very tree brought to Sri Lanka as a gift from the Buddhist Indian Emperor Ashok in the 3rd century BC, this huge specimen of *Ficus religiosa*, or sacred fig tree, has a real claim to be genuinely the oldest tree in the world. It has been guarded by an uninterrupted series of guardian monks since it was planted. It stands at the crossroads of Sri Maha Bodi Mawatha Mihindu Road and Kurunegala Road and is the best place to start exploring the sacred city.

Loha Prasada (Brazen Palace) **

A powerful imagination is needed to reconstruct this vast building, next to the sacred tree, and founded by King Dutugemunu (reigned 161–137BC). Once home to a community of 1000 Buddhist monks, whose duties included tending the sacred tree, its 1600 pillars supported nine upper storeys surmounted by a bronze roof. The whole building was decorated with silver and gems. Only the columns remain.

> ### SANGAMITTA
>
> *Sangamitta*, or *Undawap* Full Moon, usually in December, is celebrated in Sri Lanka as the day on which a sapling of the sacred bo- or **bodhi tree** under which the **Lord Buddha** attained **enlightenment** was brought to Anuradhapura by Thei Sangamitta, sister of Prince Mahindra and daughter of the Emperor Ashok. Planted in the Royal Gardens by King Devanampiyatissa, the sapling has been guarded by sentinel monks for some 2300 years and is claimed to be the oldest recorded tree in the world.

Ruwanweli Seya Dagoba ***

This dagoba is among the more impressive of Anuradhapura's monuments, if only because of its huge size. Standing 55m (180ft) tall, it was originally even taller. The base is supported by a ring of carved elephants, of which a few stone originals stand near the west door. The remainder are modern restorations. This dagoba too is the work of Dutugemunu, although he died before it could be completed.

Anuradhapura Archaeological Museum ***

The first of five new museums planned for the Cultural Triangle, the Anuradhapura Archaeological Museum, between the Brazen Palace and the Ruwanweli Seya, contains a range of exhibits discovered on the site along with explanatory displays. Among these is a model of the Thuparama Vatadage (*see* below) and a relic chamber from Mihintale (*see* page 105).

Thuparama Vatadage **

This shrine, immediately to the north of the Ruwanweli Seya, is the oldest in Sri Lanka and contains the collarbone of the Buddha, a gift from the Emperor Ashok to King Devanampiyitissa, who converted his kingdom to Buddhism. Originally built in the 3rd century BC, it has been extensively rebuilt over the centuries (most recently in 1840) and there is little to distinguish it from other dagobas around the island. It is ringed by columns which originally supported a circular roof.

IRRIGATION

The huge and complex system of tanks, aqueducts, canals and sluices which were built – often using forced labour – under the early Anuradhapura rulers were unrivalled in size and ingenuity anywhere in Asia. Great reservoirs ('tanks') were built by damming the rivers of the dry zone, some of them as much as 64km (40 miles) in circumference. From these reservoirs a network of ever smaller canals and channels fed smaller rice fields over an immense area covering hundreds of square kilometres.

Royal Palace *

About 200m (219yd) north of the Thuparama Vatadage, on the opposite side of the road, the Royal Palace ruins date from the 12th century AD, when King Vijayabahu I made a last attempt to restore some of Anuradhapura's glory and prestige. Immediately south of it is the ruin of a temple which may have been the first to house the sacred Buddha's tooth relic which now resides in Kandy and is said to have come to Sri Lanka in AD313.

Jetavanarama Dagoba and Museum ***

Looming over the entire site, the Jetavanarama Dagoba is almost 122m (400ft) tall, with a base diameter of more than 113m (370ft), putting it on a par with some of the pyramids of Egypt and making it the largest Buddhist building in southern Asia. Its core is a gigantic earthen mound, encased in brickwork, and extensive reconstruction by the UNESCO Central Cultural Fund is now nearing completion. Next to it stands the Jetavanarama Museum, housing finds from the site discovered during the reconstruction process. They include coins, Buddhist statues, seals made from precious stones, and a huge collection of beads made from clay, silver, gems, gold and ivory.

LOCAL BREWS

The poor man's intoxicant in Sri Lanka is **toddy**, produced by tapping the sugar-rich sap of the palm tree and allowing it to ferment naturally. Toddy is also distilled to produce **arrack**, a fiery white spirit which is best treated with caution and diluted with cola or fruit juice to disguise its oily taste.

Opposite: *The Ruwanweli Seya Dagoba is one of the most impressive of Anuradhapura's religious monuments.*
Below: *The Thuparama Vatadage is the country's oldest shrine and contains the Buddha's collarbone.*

THE JETAVANA TREASURES

Archaeologists working at Anuradhapura since 1981 have excavated a treasury of objects from the Jetavanarama complex that have become known as the Jetavana Treasures. They show how far-reaching were Anuradhapura's connections: there are Roman and Indian coins, ceramics from North and West Asia, and fragments of Islamic and Chinese ware. Huge numbers of beads made of clay, glass, stone, and of more precious materials such as gold, silver, ivory and carnelian have also been found, as have intaglio seals made in semiprecious stone and gold, and bronze religious statuettes.

Abhayagiri Dagoba ***

Almost as large as the Jetavanarama Dagoba is this gigantic shrine, now standing almost 110m (361ft) tall. It was built by King Abhaya in the 1st century BC and around it stood a monastery complex with a community of 5000 monks. There are exterior reliefs of elephants, and to the north of the building a stone slab is imprinted with what is said to be a footprint of the Buddha.

South of the dagoba is the Abhayagiri Museum, a gift to the people of Sri Lanka from Chinese Buddhists, which contains relics and archaeological finds illustrating the ancient connection between China and Sri Lanka. In AD412 the Chinese pilgrim Fa Hien visited Anuradhapura and wrote an account of his travels

Ratna Prasada (Gem Palace) *

Northwest of the Abhayagiri Dagoba are to be found the remnants of a 2nd century AD monastery palace of which only the mighty pillars, carved with *naga* (benevolent snake spirit) symbols, remain.

Kuttam Pokuna (Twin Ponds) **

Two lovely ritual bathing pools, fed by a stream, situated to the east of the Abhayagiri Dagoba, were once used by the monks of the Dagoba Monastery.

Samadhi Buddha Statue ***

Southeast of the Abhayagiri Dagoba, this image of a seated Buddha dates from the 4th century AD and is one of the finest of Sri Lanka's representations of the Buddha.

Southwest of the sacred bo-tree, on the shore of the Tissa Wewa tank, are several other interesting monuments.

Mirisawetiya Dagoba *

This is yet another enormous shrine, recently restored to become one of the most prominent landmarks of the sacred city.

Royal Pleasure Gardens **

Also known as the Park of the Goldfish, these gardens are a testament to the skill of the architects and landscape gardeners of Dutugemunu's reign. Covering approximately 14 ha (35 acres), they are built around ponds and rocks, with views over the Tissa Wewa tank, and were intended as a tranquil retreat from affairs of state. Some of that tranquillity survives.

Above: *The Isurumuniya Vihara is noted for its sensual friezes of embracing couples and is one of Anuradhapura's hidden secrets.*

Isurumuniya Vihara **

This rock temple, cunningly built into the crevices between great smooth basalt boulders, is one of Anuradhapura's hidden secrets. It is noted for its sensual sculptures of embracing couples, indicating a culture which, while devout, was clearly not prudish. Dating

Opposite: *The Kuttam Pokuna (Twin Ponds) were used by the monks of Anuradhapura's monasteries.*

from the 3rd century BC, it stands beside ponds above which the rock face has been carved with cheerful-looking elephants at play. More reliefs are on view inside a small museum within the temple, among them a slab that shows two lovers seated side by side and popularly said to be Saliya, son of King Dutugemunu, and his wife Asokamala. Saliya met Asokamala walking in the Pleasure Gardens, fell in love and married her. As she was not of royal blood, he forfeited his claim to the throne. It's a pretty story – but the carving, in the Gupta style of southern India in the 5th century, is more likely of a Hindu god and his queen.

Below: *White egrets and herons are seen in great numbers in Sri Lanka's rice fields, lakes and wetlands, along with many other water birds.*

WILPATTU NATIONAL PARK

Occupying about a 1100km² (425 sq mile) tract of shoreline and jungle on the northwest coast, around 180km (110 miles) north of Colombo and 50km (30 miles) west of Anuradhapura, Wilpattu is Sri Lanka's largest national park and a refuge for elephant, leopard and sloth bears. Unfortunately, its thick bush provided a refuge for LTTE fighters as well as wildlife, and it was closed to visitors in 1985. Should the risk to visitors be proven to have vanished, Wilpattu could become an ecotourism destination to rival Ruhuna in the south, with huge expanses of forest and an array of rare mammal and bird species.

SRI LANKAN BIRDS

Among the most colourful of Sri Lanka's **26 endemic bird species** is the blue magpie, with its vivid turquoise chest and back, white-barred blue tail, chestnut head and red eye and beak. Equally striking is the red-faced malkoha, with its glossy black back, wings and tail, white front, bare red pate and greenish, curved beak. The Sri Lanka jungle fowl closely resembles a domestic cockerel, with russet plumage, green-black tail feathers and a red comb and wattle. An unusual species is the Sri Lankan hanging parrot, with a red cap, yellow nape and bright green wings and breast, which, instead of perching normally on a branch, hangs upside down.

Anuradhapura and the Northwest at a Glance

The northwest is most pleasant from September to late April. From May to September the **southwest monsoon** brings heavy rainfall.

By Rail: Trains from Colombo to Anuradhapura and Kaduruwela (for Polonnaruwa).
By Bus: Direct buses from Colombo to Anuradhapura and Kaduruwela (for Polonnaruwa). Direct buses from Kandy to Dambulla and Anuradhapura via the A9/A13 highway, and Polonnaruwa.

Local buses connect all points in the area. Taxis are available in Polonnaruwa, Anuradhapura and other towns. Taxi fares should be agreed with the driver before boarding.

Luxury hotels in the region are to be found at Giritale, between Polonnaruwa and Sigiriya, and at Dambulla. Mid-range accommodation is easy to find, but budget accommodation is thinner on the ground, with most budget places to stay in the Anuradhapura and Polonnaruwa areas.

Habarana
LUXURY
The Lodge, Habarana, tel: (066) 8316, fax: (066) 70046. Scenic hotel resort with 150 luxury chalets set in a lush woodland setting.

MID-RANGE
The Village, Habarana, tel: (066) 8321, fax: (066) 70011. Comfortable chalet complex with 106 rooms in 12 acres of lawns and flowering trees.

Polonnaruwa Area
LUXURY
Deer Park Hotel, Giritale, Polonnaruwa, tel: (027) 46470, fax: (01) 448848. Quality hotel with pool, health centre, Sri Lankan speciality restaurant, gym, tennis and herbal health centre.

MID-RANGE
Giritale Hotel, National Holiday Resort, Giritale, Polonnaruwa, tel: (027) 46311, fax: (027) 46086. Comfortable air-conditioned rooms, sauna, pool, fishing and boat trips, lake views.

BUDGET
Royal Lotus Hotel, Giritale, Polonnaruwa, tel: (027) 46316, fax: (027) 448849. Very good value, with air-conditioned rooms, pool, nature walks, wildlife safaris.
The Village, Polonnaruwa, tel: (027) 22405, fax: (027) 23366. A 36-room hotel with air conditioning, three family rooms, bar, TV room and swimming pool.
Hotel Seruwa, Polonnaruwa, tel: (027) 22411, fax: (027) 22412. Small hotel with swimming pool, 3km (1.8 miles) from Polonnaruwa town.

Sigiriya
MID-RANGE
Sigiriya Village Hotel, PO Box 1, Sigiriya, tel: (066) 31803, fax: (066) 23502. This hotel has pool, tennis and badminton courts.

Anuradhapura
MID-RANGE
Tissawewa Resthouse, Old Town, Anuradhapura, tel: (025) 22299, fax: (025) 23265. Close to the lake and the archaeological site. Bikes for hire. Comfortable rooms.

BUDGET
Ashok Hotel, 20 Rowing Club Road, Anuradhapura, tel and fax: (025) 22753. Good value, comfortable hotel in the new town.

Generally, the best places to eat in the northwest are in the hotels listed.

Several holiday hotels in the region, including the Giritale Hotel, National Holiday Resort, Giritale, tel: (027) 46311, fax: (027) 46086, and the Culture Club Resort, PO Box 12, Kandalama, Dambulla, tel: (066) 23500, fax: (0722) 44360, offer such excursions as boat trips, elephant safaris and jeep safaris, boat and fishing trips.

7
Trincomalee, the East Coast and the North

Tourism has barely touched the beautiful beaches of Sri Lanka's east coast, and its national parks are hardly visited. With no international airport in easy reach, the eastern part of the country was less attractive than the south and west when sun, sea and sand tourism first began. Since then, the region, whose population is divided between Sinhalese, Tamil and Muslim communities, has been drawn into the **civil war** between armed Tamil insurgents and government forces. It is now in theory possible to visit Trincomalee, though the journey involves passing through frequent military checkpoints, and non-residents may well be refused permission to travel at the whim of the Sri Lankan security forces. If you are contemplating visiting this part of the country, take advice from your country's embassy in Colombo before doing so and pay attention to local advice from security forces within the area.

Sri Lanka's east coast has long stretches of beach, some of it good for surfing and diving, while large expanses of the hill country that roll towards the coast from the central highlands are protected by national parks (both, sadly, off limits at present). Two major towns, **Trincomalee** in the north and **Batticaloa** midway along the coast, stand guard over the region's two natural harbours, and large stretches of the coast are deserted except for small fishing communities. Sri Lanka's largest river, the **Mahaweli Ganga**, which flows though Kandy from a source in the southwest highlands, reaches the sea at Koddiyar Bay, south of Trincomalee.

INDIAN OCEAN

Opposite: *Swami Rock towers above Trincomalee's waterfront.*

CLIMATE

The east coast's rainy season is from October to January, with rainfall reaching more than 350mm (14in) in November and December. Rainfall is well below 100mm (4in) from February to July, and slightly above this level in August and September. Maximum temperatures reach almost 35°C (95°F) from April to September, dropping below 30°C (86°F) only for the remaining six months of the year, with an **average temperature** of **26°C–30°C** (79–86°F) all the year round.

Trincomalee

Nilaveli
Uppuveli
Trincomalee ①②
④ *Foul Point*
Mutur

1. Fort Frederick
2. Swami Rock
3. Fort Ostenburg
4. Koddiyar Bay
5. Dutch Settlement
6. Maha Oya Hot Spring
7. Arugam Bay

Mahaweli Ganga
Trikonamadu Natural Reserve
Trikonamadu

0   20 km
0   10 miles   N

A15   *Elephant Point*

Trikkandimadu

Eastern Province
Eravur
Batticaloa
Maduru Oya National Park   A5   Kattankudi
Maha Oya   A27   A4
658 m ▲
Wedihiti Hela (Friar's Hood)   Kalmunai
Ampara
Senanayake Samudra   Akkaraipattu
Gal Oya National Park   A25
Sakamam
Province of Uva   Lahugala National Park
Tennugewatta
Monaragala   Pottuvil ⑦
A4
YALA NATIONAL PARK

TRINCOMALEE

The region's largest city stands on an isthmus with two deep bays to seaward and a fine natural Inner Harbour to the west. It naturally attracted the attention of European colonial powers as early as the first quarter of the 17th century, changing hands repeatedly among the Portuguese, the Dutch, the French and the British in a series of side-shows to the European wars of the 17th and 18th centuries, before finally falling to a British fleet in 1795. It remained one of the British Empire's most important ports in Asia, and from 1941–45 was the headquarters of the Allied Southeast Asia commander, Lord Louis Mountbatten. Other distinguished British military men to have sojourned here include Sir Arthur Wellesley (later the Duke of Wellington), who recuperated here in 1799 from fever caught while campaigning against the French and their allies in southern India. In the middle of the Inner Harbour, connected to the isthmus by a narrow causeway, is Powder Island, once a gunpowder magazine for the Royal Navy, but now occupied by the Sri Lankan defence force.

Fort Frederick *

The northeast-pointing promontory which separates Dutch Bay from Back Bay was fortified first by the Portuguese, then by their successors and finally by the British, who named it Fort Frederick. It is now in the hands of the Sri Lankan military, so access is problematic. At the tip of the promontory is Swami Rock, where a Hindu temple stood until being demolished by the Portuguese.

Trincomalee Beaches *

Uppuveli is the most conveniently located beach for those staying in Trincomalee, only 6km (4 miles) north of the city centre and accessible by taxi or three-wheeler. Nilaveli is a 4km (2.5-mile) stretch of beach which starts about 16km (10 miles) north of Trincomalee and which, until the troubles, was poised to become one of the east coast's first mid-range resort areas.

Above: *Temples and fortifications at Swami Rock.*
Opposite: *Fishing boat on Nilaveli beach.*

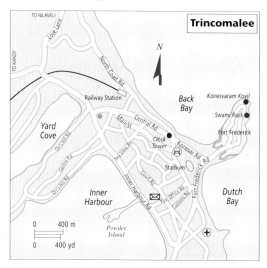

Trincomalee map showing: TO NILAVELI, Love Lane, TO KANDY, North Coast Rd, Railway Station, Back Bay, Koneswaram Kovil, Swami Rock, Yard Cove, Main St, Central Rd, Clock Tower, Konesar Rd, Fort Frederick, Sea View Rd, Dockyard Rd, Centre Rd, Stadium, Court Rd, Inner Harbour, Inner Harbour Rd, Post Office Rd, Fort Frederick Rd, Customs Rd, Dutch Bay, Powder Island.

0   400 m
0   400 yd

BATTICALOA AND ENVIRONS

The second largest town on the east coast, Batticaloa stands on a long, sandy spit of land pointing northward and separated from the mainland by a large brackish lagoon which extends southward for many kilometres. This location made it easy for the LTTE, which seized control of the town in the 1980s, to defend it against government forces, and the guerrillas were not expelled until 1991. As in the area of Jaffna, the larger Tamil stronghold in the extreme north, the security forces succeeded in retaking the town, only for the LTTE to fade into the countryside, which remains highly unsafe for travellers.

Pottuvil and Arugam Bay

Below: *Jaffna lagoon is off limits to tourists, and to any vessel more sophisticated than these primitive fishing boats.*

Arugam Bay, 3km (2 miles) south of the small fishing village of Pottuvil, had a reputation as a surfer's paradise before the area became unsafe due to incidents in and around Pottuvil and on the roads leading to it. It has long, empty beaches and a wide lagoon which is a haven for numerous bird species.

DEEPAVALI

Deepavali, the **Festival of Lights**, is one of the most important festivals of the **Hindu** year. Held in November, it is dedicated to Lakshmi, goddess of wealth and consort of Vishnu. Lakshmi appears with Vishnu in all his reincarnations, and as Sita, wife of Rama, was kidnapped by the demon king of Lanka, starting the great war between gods and demons recounted in the epic *Ramayana*.

Left: *Lahugala National Park has the country's biggest concentration of elephants during the dry season.*

Lahugala National Park

About 16km (10 miles) west of Pottuvil, Lahugala was designated as a national park mainly to provide a protected corridor for elephant groups moving between the larger reserves of Ruhuna (Yala), to the south, and Gal Oya, to the north. In the dry season this small park is reputed to have more elephants than any other part of the country, attracted by the grazing around the reservoirs within the park.

Below: *Batticaloa's large, brackish lagoon is rich in fish, prawns and other sea creatures and because of the troubles is largely unexploited except by local fishers.*

Gal Oya National Park

Gal Oya covers 260km² (100 sq miles) of scrub and open country around an artificial reservoir, the Senanayake Samudra (Senanayake Sea), named after Sri Lanka's first post-independence prime minister. Formed in the early 1950s by damming the Gal Oya River, which flows out of the foothills to feed the lagoons south of Batticaloa, the huge lake has a deeply indented coastline, suitable for exploring and viewing game by boat. Unfortunately it is closed until further notice.

JAFFNA AND THE NORTH

The arid north of Sri Lanka, terminating in the Jaffna Peninsula, which points west towards the tip of India, is the country's Tamil heartland and has been the focus of the horrific civil war of the 1980s and 1990s. The LTTE was driven out of its strongholds in Jaffna and other towns and villages in government offensives from 1995 onward, but remained a force to be reckoned with, and travel throughout the north was presumed unsafe at the time of going to press. In comparison with the rich tourism pickings of southern and central Sri Lanka, Jaffna and the north and east have relatively little to offer the average visitor.

Should travel to the region again become possible, a sight worth seeing is the **Jaffna Fort**, built by the Dutch to command the lagoon. A typical star fort of the late 18th century, it covers an area of more than 20ha (49 acres) and has remained a military garrison until the present day – until 1995 the only government garrison in the north was besieged within its walls by the LTTE and could be supplied only with difficulty by air and sea.

Delft, named after the Dutch town, is an island 35km (22 miles) from Jaffna, with another small Dutch fort. **Mannar Island**, linked to the mainland by a 3km (2-mile) causeway, is the westernmost point of Sri Lanka, and is at one end of 'Adam's Bridge', the line of rocks, shoals and islands dotted between India and Sri Lanka. In happier times a ferry connected Sri Lanka to the subcontinent.

Trincomalee, the East Coast and the North at a Glance

Despite the country's small size, Sri Lanka's west and east coasts have distinctly different weather patterns. The north and east are affected by the northeast monsoon, from November to February, but are at their finest between May and September, when the rest of the country is experiencing the heavy rain, wind and surf brought by the southwest monsoon season. An improvement in the security situation, making it safe for tourists to visit the region's beaches, would make Sri Lanka a year-round holiday destination.

GETTING THERE

By rail: To Trincomalee from Colombo once daily via Habarana (7–8 hr).
By bus: To Trincomalee from Colombo (7 hr), Kandy (5 hr), Anuradhapura (4 hr) and Habarana (2–3 hr).
Travel to the Jaffna Peninsula was not permitted at the time of going to press.

GETTING AROUND

Three-wheelers, buses and taxis operate within Trincomalee and in both directions up and down the coast. Be aware that travel may be interrupted at any time, depending on the security situation.

WHERE TO STAY

Due to the security situation, with travel restricted through-

out most of the region, it is not possible to recommend hotels or restaurants outside the immediate area of Trincomalee. Finding anything but the most basic budget accommodation is likely to be a challenge as the handful of larger hotels on the east coast's fledgling resort beaches have mostly closed for lack of business. Should peace and security return fully, smaller hotels are likely to reopen first.

Trincomalee and around

There are no luxury properties in Trincomalee; the only hotel which approaches mid-range levels of comfort is the Nilaveli.

MID-RANGE

Nilaveli Beach Hotel, 11th Mile Post, Nilaveli, Trincomalee, tel: (026) 22071, fax: (026) 448279. Slightly run-down but with an excellent location on the beach at Nilaveli. Air-conditioned rooms available.

BUDGET

Shahira Hotel, 10th Mile Post, Nilaveli, Trincomalee, tel: (026) 32224.
The Villa, 22 Orr's Hill Road, Trincomalee, tel: (026) 22284.

Comfortable guesthouse with own restaurant and en-suite accommodation.
Hotel New Sea Lord, 3rd Mile Post, Uppuveli, Trincomalee, tel: (026) 22396, no fax. Reasonably comfortable small hotel on the nearest beach to Trincomalee town.

WHERE TO EAT

All the hotels listed above have simple restaurants serving Sri Lankan dishes and seafood. Food stalls and basic restaurants can be found in Trincomalee. Elsewhere, eating places are likely to be cheap and simple.

USEFUL CONTACTS

Advice from the British Foreign and Commonwealth Office at the time of going to press was for travellers to avoid the entire northern and eastern part of the country. Although no immediate end to the trouble was in sight in early 2000, the situation could change. For updated advice and information on travel to Sri Lanka, check the Foreign and Commonwealth Office website: www.fco.gov.uk/ or consult your travel agent.

EAST COAST	J	F	M	A	M	J	J	A	S	O	N	D
AVERAGE TEMP. °C	26	26	27	29	30	30	30	30	30	28	27	26
AVERAGE TEMP. °F	78	79	81	84	86	86	85	85	85	82	80	78
HOURS OF SUN DAILY	7	9	9	9	8	7	7	7	8	6	6	6
RAINFALL mm	133	66	48	58	69	28	51	107	107	221	358	363
RAINFALL in	6.8	2.6	1.9	2.3	2.7	1.1	2	4.2	4.2	8.7	14.1	14.3
DAYS OF RAINFALL	10	4	4	5	5	2	3	6	6	13	17	16

Travel Tips

Tourist Information

Though the country changed its name in 1972, tourism information is still provided by the Ceylon Tourist Board with offices worldwide. These offices are:

United Kingdom: Ceylon Tourist Board, Trade Centre, 22 Regent Street, London SW1Y, tel: (0171) 930 2627/9070.

Canada: Ceylon Tourist Board, Cathedral Place, 925 West Georgic Street, Vancouver BC, Canada V6C 3L2, tel: (0604) 688 8528.

Ireland: Ceylon Tourist Board, 59 Ranelagh Road, Dublin 6, tel: (01) 496 5345.

Australia: Ceylon Tourist Board, Atutil Pty. Ltd, 39 Wintercorn Row, Werrington Downs, NSW Australia 2747.

Germany: Ceylon Tourist Board, Allerheilgentor 2–4, D-6000 Frankfurt/ Main 1, tel: (069) 287734.

In other countries, information and tourism literature may be obtained from the Sri Lankan embassy or high commission.

Within **Sri Lanka**:
Ceylon Tourist Board, 80 Galle Road, Colombo 3, tel: (01) 437059.

Entry Requirements

Visas are not required by nationals of the USA, UK, Canada, Australia, New Zealand, Germany and most other British Commonwealth and European Union nations. Your passport should have at least six months' validity on arrival.

Sri Lankan Embassies, Consulates and High Commissions:

United Kingdom: 13 Hyde Park Gardens, London W2 2LU, tel: (0171) 262 1841.

United States of America: 2148 Wyoming Avenue NW, Washington DC 20008, tel: (202) 483 4026.

Australia: 35 Empire Circuit, Forrest, Canberra, ACT 2603, tel: (06) 239 7401.

Canada: Suite 1204, 333 Lauries Avenue West, Ottawa, Ontario K1P 1Cl, tel: (613) 233 84409.

Germany: Noeggerathstrasse 15, 53111, Bonn 2, tel: (0228) 698 946.

Customs

You may import one and a half litres (approx three pints/two bottles) of spirits, two bottles of wine, 200 cigarettes or 50 cigars. Banned goods include gold; Sri Lanka currency in excess of Rs 250; firearms, explosives or other weapons; antiques; animals, birds or reptiles; tea, rubber and coconut plants; dangerous drugs. Gems, jewellery and 'valuable goods' – such as video recorders and personal computers – must be declared on arrival.

Health Requirements

Immunization against hepatitis A, polio and typhoid is recommended. Malaria and cholera are present and a malaria preventative is recommended especially if travelling during the wet season. Take medical advice before travelling.

Getting There

By Air: Main flight connections from Europe are by Air Lanka from London, Frankfurt, Paris, Stockholm,

Zurich and Rome to Colombo. Air Lanka also has connections to Delhi, Mumbai (Bombay), Madras, Maldives, Singapore, Bangkok, Kuala Lumpur, Hong Kong, Tokyo, and Sydney. Other carriers include British Airways, Aeroflot (via Moscow), Bulgarian Airlines (via Sofia), Royal Jordanian (via Amman), and Emirates (via Dubai).
By Sea: Some cruise lines, including Swan Hellenic, offer cruise and tour combinations with tours of the ancient cities as part of a cruise itinerary.

What to Pack

For men: light cotton or linen short-sleeved shirts, and/or T-shirts, shorts and light baggy pants for the coast, lightweight linen suit for business or more formal occasions, light jacket or cotton sweatshirt for evenings in Kandy and the hills where evenings can be cooler. Jacket and tie required at some older, more formal hotel restaurants and clubs.
For women: linen or cotton skirts, tops, pants; shorts and T-shirts; beachwear. For business, tailored linen dress or suit. Large cotton or silk shawl comes in handy for cool up-country evenings.
For both: modest wear covering knees, arms and shoulders is required for visiting temples, mosques and sacred sites, including the ancient cities. Other useful items: Swiss Army

knife or similar, small torch and batteries, mosquito repellent, binoculars.

Money Matters

The Sri Lankan rupee is divided into 100 cents. Coins come in denominations of 5, 10, 25 and 50 cents and 1, 2, 5 and 10 rupees. Notes are denominated in values of 10, 20, 50, 100, 500 and 1000. When changing money, ask for smaller denomination notes as merchants, taxi drivers and three-wheeler drivers are often mysteriously unable to give change.

Tipping

Universal but modest; a few rupees or even cents in more basic places will be welcomed.

Accommodation

Colombo offers a wide range of accommodation from international brand five-star hotels to basic guesthouses. Elsewhere, there are high-quality resort hotels in resorts north and south of the capital, especially in Negombo, Beruwala and Bentota, and at Hikkaduwa. Inland, there are comfortable hotels at Kandy, and mid-range hotels close to the ancient cities of Polonnaruwa and Anuradhapura. Elsewhere, there are numerous small family-run guesthouses and hotels which offer basic but very affordable accommodation. Many of these, while simple, are very clean, friendly

ROAD SIGNS

Road signs are in English, with distances in kilometres. Street signs and most shop and office signs are also in English, though many are in Sinhala, or less frequently in Tamil.

and well-run and can offer surprisingly good value for money. This is true too at the top of the range, as Sri Lanka's supply of luxury and mid-range hotel beds considerably outstrips demand. In some places there are rest-houses, built by the colonial powers for travelling administrators and now mostly operated by the Ceylon Hotel Corporation, 411 Galle Road, Colombo 4, tel: (072) 52575. These are often comfortable, atmospheric and evocative of a bygone era.

Eating Out

Sri Lanka has plenty of restaurants, ranging from smart Colombo nightspots catering to the country's better off to the simplest of beach bars. At resorts, major hotels usually offer a choice of international-style and Sri Lankan buffet meals, while around the main hotel complexes at Negombo, Bentota, Beruwala and Hikkaduwa independent restaurants have mushroomed, offering a range of cuisine that reflects the main tourism sources – Britain, Germany, Italy and Switzerland. The main hotels in Colombo have several restaurants each, usually offering Japanese, Sri Lankan, and Euro-international fare. Many smaller, cheaper restaurants around the country offer a choice of Sri Lankan curries and the Sri Lankan version of Chinese rice and noodle dishes like chow mein. Across the board, restaurant prices are very affordable by inter-national standards, though drinking imported beers and especially imported wines will push the bill up sharply.

Transport

Air: There is no internal air network.

Trains: Sri Lanka has an extensive rail network and it is possible to get to most of the key places to visit by rail. Some trains offer first, second and third class, some only second and third, some only first and second. In addition, some trains offer air conditioning in first class, while those on the overnight run from Colombo to Badulla offer sleeperettes.
Some trains on the highly scenic stretch between

Colombo and Kandy have observation car berths.
Buses: State-operated and privately-run buses link Colombo with all points and operate between major towns. They are almost always crowded, uncomfortable, and at times dangerous due to minimum maintenance and reckless driving. Rail travel is preferable whenever possible.
Car hire: Self-drive car hire is available but extreme caution should be used when driving on Sri Lanka's roads, due to poor road surfaces. Standards of driving are low and many vehicles, especially buses and lorries, may not be well maintained. Cars with drivers can be hired from travel agencies in Colombo and at resorts, and taxis can be hired by negotiating a daily rate with the driver.

Business Hours

Banks normally open 09:00–13:00. Most government and commercial offices open 08:30 to 16:30. Shops open 08:00 or 09:00 to 19:00 Monday to Friday,

closing early afternoon on Saturdays. Most Buddhist and Hindu temples and shrines are open from dawn until nightfall.

Time Difference

GMT +55 hours 30 minutes.

Communications

Post offices open Monday–Friday 08:00–17:00. Government post offices exist in all towns and villages and there are also private 'agency' post offices in most larger towns. Telephone calls throughout Sri Lanka are almost all direct dial; if direct dial is not yet available, dial 101 for trunk call connections. **International Direct Dial** (IDD) is available. For international enquiries, tel: 134 within Colombo or (01) 324144/329792 outside Colombo. You can make international direct dial calls and send express mail **faxes**, telegrams and **electronic mail** from the new post office at 1st Floor, World Trade Centre East Tower, Colombo 1.
Prepaid **telephone cards** can be bought from post offices and shops near telephone boxes.

Electricity

230–240V, 50 cycle AC, three-round-pin sockets.

Weights and Measures

Sri Lanka uses the metric system of measurement.

Health Precautions

You must have comprehen-

CONVERSION CHART		
FROM	**TO**	**MULTIPLY BY**
Millimetres	Inches	0.0394
Metres	Yards	1.0936
Metres	Feet	3.281
Kilometres	Miles	0.6214
Square kilometres	Square miles	0.386
Hectares	Acres	2.471
Litres	Pints	1.760
Kilograms	Pounds	2.205
Tonnes	Tons	0.984
To convert Celsius to Fahrenheit: x 9 ÷ 5 + 32		

sive **health insurance** and take professional medical advice on immunizations several months before travelling to Sri Lanka. Immunizations worth considering include hepatitis A, Japanese encephalitis and typhoid. Malaria prophylaxis is advisable and mosquito repellent is essential. **Do not drink tap water** anywhere in Sri Lanka unless you have boiled or sterilized it yourself. Carry water sterilizing tablets, available from chemists in the UK and elsewhere, if you are heading off the beaten track where bottled drinks may not be available. Food is generally safer than in some other countries in the Asian subcontinent, but you must use your own judgement in deciding whether a restaurant or food stall looks (and smells) acceptably clean. Many travellers in Sri Lanka avoid meat and settle for cooked vegetarian food, which may carry fewer risks. However, Sri Lanka's delicious seafood is hard to resist. Pack Immodium or a similar preparation to alleviate symptoms of diarrhoea, as well as electrolyte mix for rehydration. Sunburn and heat exhaustion are significant risks at all times of year and children, especially, should be kept out of the sun as much as possible. Drink plenty of water to minimize dehydration. Even small cuts and scrapes can become infected. Wash carefully and then apply antiseptic.

Health Services
Most luxury and mid-range hotels have a doctor on call. Your travel insurance should include emergency repatriation. **General Hospital Emergency Services**, 10 Regent Street, Colombo 8, tel: (01) 691111.

Personal Safety
British Foreign and Commonwealth Office travel advice in force at the time of going to press was that the north and east of Sri Lanka should not be visited. Between 1995 and 1999 more than 350 people were killed and 2000 wounded in serious bomb attacks in Colombo. These were not aimed specifically at tourists, but further unpredictable and indiscriminate attacks cannot be ruled out.

Most of Sri Lanka, including the major cultural centres, the hill country and the coastal tourist resorts, remained unaffected by the ethnic violence.

Apart from politically inspired violence, incidents of violent crime against tourists are rare, but theft is more common. Do not leave passports, cash, traveller's cheques, tickets or other valuables in your room – carry them with you in a secure money belt or concealed pouch, or put them in a hotel safe or deposit box. Keep a close watch on your possessions when travelling by public transport. Reporting theft at police stations is a time-consuming bureaucratic process. Use of soft drugs by budget travellers is not uncommon.

PUBLIC HOLIDAYS & FESTIVALS

Sri Lanka marks the main
Buddhist, Hindu, Muslim and
some Christian festivals as
public holidays.
Many of these are
moveable feasts,
the precise date depending
on phases of the moon.
January 1 • Duruthu Poya
Day/New Year's Day
January 15 • Tamil Thai
Pongal Day
January/February • Id Ul Fitr
(Ramazan Festival Day)
February 4 • National Day
March • Id Ul Allah
(Haj Festival Day)
April • Good Friday
April • Sinhalese
and Tamil New Year
May 1 • May Day
June • Milad Un Nabi
(Holy Prophet's Birthday)
November • Deepavali
(Hindu Festival of Lights)
25 December •
Christmas Day

You may be approached
by drug dealers. Be aware
that possession of cannabis
or other drugs carries heavy
penalties.

Emergencies

Police: (01) 433333.
Fire: (01) 422222.
Tourist Police: (01) 327711.

Etiquette

Sri Lankans of every faith
value modesty. Beachwear is
acceptable at beach resorts,
less acceptable off the beach
and wholly unacceptable at
temples, mosques and
shrines. Footwear and head-
gear must be removed
before entering Buddhist or
Hindu shrines. Posing beside
or on religious statues is
prohibited. Topless and
nude sunbathing are illegal.

Language

Sri Lanka is a land of several
languages, and language is a
political issue. Early attempts
at making Sinhalese (or
Sinhala) the sole language of
government and education
sparked the first Tamil
protests in the early 1970s.
Both Sinhala (spoken by
more than 70 per cent of Sri
Lankans) and Tamil (spoken
by around 20 per cent) now
have the status of 'national'
languages, while Sinhala is
the 'official' language.
English, which is widely
spoken and used on signs,
maps, timetables and place
names, provides a neutral
link between the two.

Shopping

Sri Lanka is a treasure house
of riches for the souvenir
shopper, with mementoes to
suit all budgets. Small craft
and souvenir shops surround
virtually every resort hotel,
and bargaining is the order
of the day. At the lower end
of the scale, there are carved
wooden masks depicting
nagas and other mythical
characters from the Sri
Lankan pantheon of demons
and deities. Leather goods
such as bags and belts are
also good value. The quality
and price of silver and gold
jewellery depends on the
workmanship and the gold
and silver content. Precious
and semi-precious gemstones
are widely sold, especially
around Ratnapura, Sri Lanka's
'gem city'. The most valuable
are rubies and sapphires.
Beware, however, of buying
gems on the street or of
dealers who offer a seemingly
irresistible bargain – invariably,
on returning home, the stone
you have bought will turn out
to be worth far less than you
paid for it, and may be completely worthless. Reputable
gem centres in Colombo are
the only reliable place to buy
stones. Avoid buying goods
made from ivory, turtle shell,
or reptile skin of any kind.
Local vendors may assure you
that such wild animal products
are legal in Sri Lanka or are
made from spcies which are
not endangered. This is
unlikely to be true (there are
no snake or other reptile
farms in Sri Lanka) and your
new purchases will be con-
fiscated by customs on your
return home.

GOOD READING

Roberts, Karen (1999) The Flower Boy, Orion
Clarke, Arthur C, The View from Serendip
Ondaatje, Michael, Running in the Family, Penguin
Woolf, Leonard (1981) The Village in the Jungle,
Oxford University Press
Wijeyeratne, Gehan de Silva et al (1997) Birdwatcher's Guide to
Sri Lanka, Oriental Bird Club

INDEX

Note: Numbers in **bold** indicate photographs